Southwick's Mira
The day a Valian

By

Mary Candy

Published by the Southwick (Sussex) Society

Copyright © Mary Candy

ISBN 978-1-9164045-1-9

All rights reserved. No portion of this book may be reproduced, stored in a retrieval system or transmitted at any time or by any means mechanical, electronic, photocopying, recording or otherwise, without the prior, written permission of the publisher.

The right of Mary Candy to be identified as the author of this work has been asserted by her in accordance with the Copyright, Designs and Patents act 1988.

Printed by Fairhall & Bryant Printers Ltd

First printed 2021

Cover picture: The first prototype Vickers Valiant at the Farnborough Airshow, *1951*, courtesy Aircraft Engine Historical Society, Inc., http://www.enginehistory.org

Contents

Introduction 3
Background 3
   The Vickers Valiant bomber 3
   The Ministry of Supply and the Royal Aircraft Establishment 5
   The experimental test programme 5
Part One: The Crash 7
   The test flight 7
   The accident investigation 10
   The Court of Inquiry 14
      Expert witnesses 18
      Valiant WP 202's previous flight 20
      Civilian witnesses 23
      Evidence of MOT Accidents Investigation Branch and RAE Accidents Investigation Section 26
      Valiants grounded 30
      Court findings 32
   The Inquest 35
Part Two: The Impact on the Local Community 37
   Destroyed homes and miraculous escapes 37
   Eyewitness accounts 48
   Press attention 51
   The aftermath 58
   Protests against low flying jets 62
Part Three: The Wider Picture 66
   British Soviet relations 66
   Dangerous times in the skies 67
   Ejector seats for the rear crew 68
   Fred Jones' crash investigation book 70
   Flight Lieutenant Colin Preece's later account of the crash 72
Final Thoughts 73
Glossary 76
Acknowledgements 77

A map of Southwick showing the crash location.

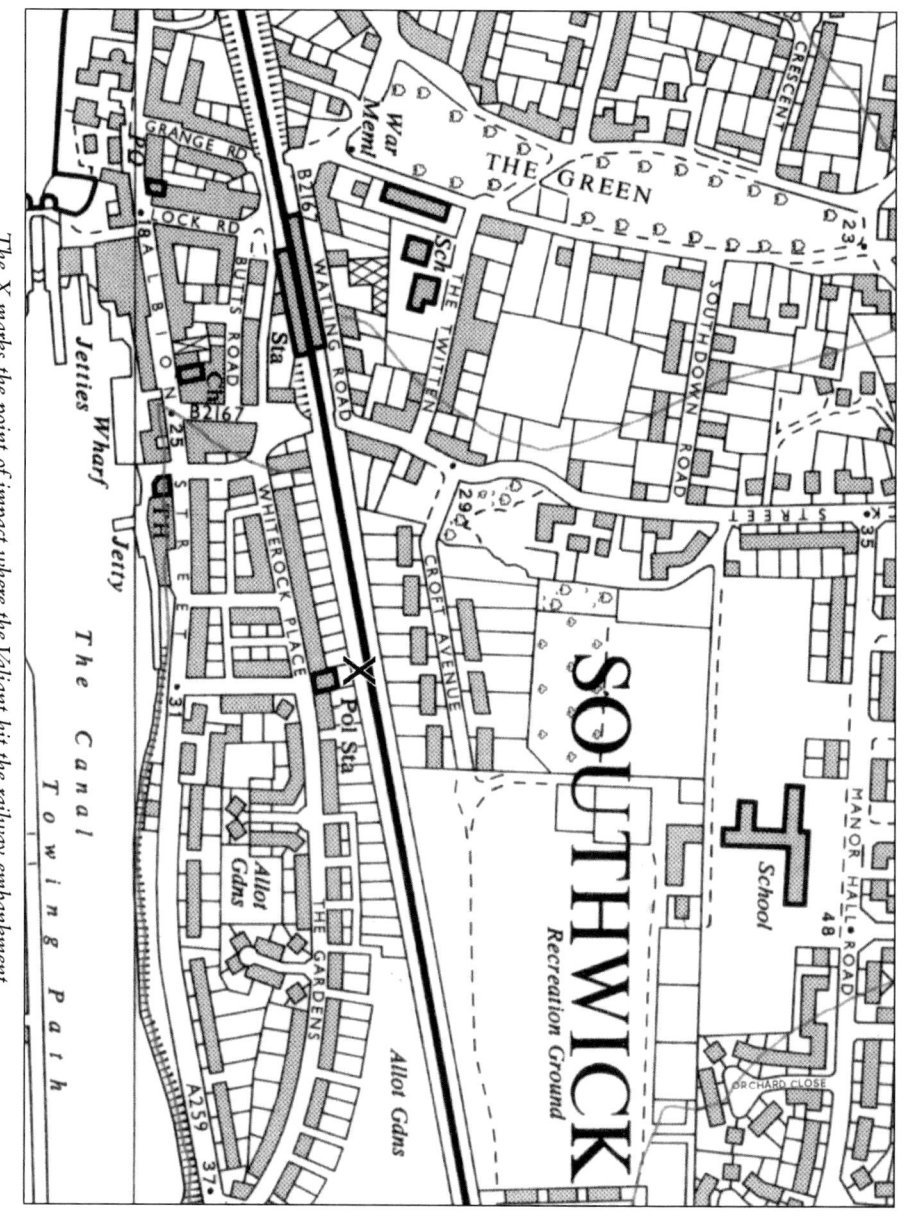

The X marks the point of impact where the Valiant hit the railway embankment

Introduction

In 1956 the Second World War was still a recent memory; rationing had only ended two years previously and jet aeroplanes were still relatively new. The perceived threat from Soviet Russia was growing and the Cold War was beginning. Britain was establishing its nuclear deterrent and the development of the Valiant bomber was part of that deterrent. Imagine then the shock in a small village in West Sussex when one of these new bombers, Valiant B Mk 1 WP 202, crashed on to the embankment of the railway line and strewed its wreckage over the local recreation ground. Some residents even feared that the plane may actually have been carrying a nuclear bomb when it crashed. Southwick was suddenly in the news.

Despite the gravity of the accident and the impact it had on the people of Southwick there is no permanent record locally of what happened. Naturally the investigation into the crash was carried out behind closed doors and the resulting report was classified 'Secret'. So, although many residents I have spoken to remember the crash and the wreckage on the Recreation Ground, none of them know any details about what the aircraft was doing or what caused the accident. In 1988 the Accident Investigation Board documents were declassified and are now available to view at The National Archives in Kew.

I have used the documents from The National Archives, together with newspaper reports and eyewitness accounts, to put together this record of what happened to an almost new Valiant bomber on Friday 11th May 1956 and how it affected the local people and community.

Background

The Vickers Valiant bomber

Post war Britain was very concerned about the nuclear threat from the Soviet Union. A new type of bomber was required which could be equipped with nuclear weapons, as part of Britain's strategic deterrent. The bomber needed to be able to carry a 10,000lb atomic bomb to a target 1,725 miles away, from a base anywhere in the world. The aircraft was required to deliver its bomb deep into enemy territory and avoid destruction by enemy aircraft or anti-aircraft defences. Four companies put forward designs: A V Roe and Company (Avro), Handley Page Ltd, Vickers-Armstrong Ltd, and Shorts Brothers and Harland Ltd. Avro and Handley Page put forward two very innovative designs, while the other two were simpler and less risky. It was decided to proceed with the Vickers' safer design, while Avro and Handley Page would also develop their riskier aircraft. All three of these designs were a massive technological advance over the existing heavy bombers, the Lancaster and the Lincoln. The V-bombers as they became known, because of their names, Valiant, Vulcan and Victor, were developed in parallel with Britain's first atomic bomb, the Blue Danube. This was a free-fall plutonium bomb and required a larger bomb bay than was available on the new Canberra, Britain's first jet bomber, which had come into service in 1950.

A prototype of the Vickers plane, WB 210, first flew on 18th May 1951, and in June 1951 the plane was given the name Valiant. In April 1951 the Ministry of Supply had placed an order for 25 Valiant B1 (Bomber Mark 1) aircraft on behalf of the Royal Air Force. It was a conventional high-wing aircraft with four Rolls Royce jet engines. The wings were mounted on the shoulder of the fuselage, which allowed a huge bomb bay to be included. The Valiant entered service in June 1954 and on 1st January 1955 the first Valiant squadron, No. 138, was formed at RAF Gaydon. An Operational Conversion Unit, 232, was formed at Gaydon on 21 February 1955 to convert pilots to fly the new bomber. Since the Valiant was part of an entirely new class of bomber for the RAF, the crews were selected from experienced aircrew, with first pilots requiring 1,750 flying hours as an aircraft captain, with at least one tour flying the Canberra. Second pilots needed 700 hours in command and the remaining three crew members had to be recommended for posting to the Valiant by their commanding officers.

Vickers Valiant WP 215, the second prototype had its maiden flight on 11th April 1952. Photo by Neil Aird

On 11th October 1956 Valiant B.1 WZ 366 dropped a Blue Danube bomb from an altitude of 35,000ft over Maralinga in Australia as part of a test. This was the first air drop of a British nuclear weapon. Also in October 1956 Valiant bombers dropped conventional bombs during the Suez crisis. On 15th May 1957 a Valiant dropped a prototype hydrogen bomb from 39,000ft as part of the Christmas Islands hydrogen bomb tests. The Valiant was later also developed to be used as a long-range reconnaissance plane with cameras replacing the bombs.

By the early 1960s the Soviet's air defences had become too effective against high-level nuclear bombers and V-bombers were switched to low level operations. However, the Valiants suffered serious stress fractures from the low-level flying and the fleet was grounded and then withdrawn from service in January 1965.

The Ministry of Supply and the Royal Aircraft Establishment

The Ministry of Supply (MoS) was a Government department formed in 1939 to co-ordinate the supply of equipment to all three British armed forces. After the war, in 1946, they took over responsibility for aircraft research establishments including The Royal Aircraft Establishment based at Farnborough in Hampshire. In the same year the MoS took on increased responsibilities for atomic weapons, including the H-bomb development programme.

The Royal Aircraft Establishment (RAE) began life as the Army Balloon Factory and in 1906 it moved from Aldershot to the edge of Farnborough Common, where there was enough space to inflate the new "dirigible balloon" or airship which was then under construction. On 16th October 1908 Samuel Franklin Cody made the first aeroplane flight in Britain at Farnborough. In 1912 the Balloon Factory was renamed the Royal Aircraft Factory (RAF). Its first new designer was Geoffrey de Havilland who later founded his own company. In 1918 the Royal Aircraft Factory was once more renamed, becoming the Royal Aircraft Establishment (RAE) to avoid confusion with the Royal Air Force, which had been formed on 1 April 1918, and also because it had stopped manufacturing to concentrate on research.

The experimental test programme

As more Valiants came into operation existing jet pilots were given training to convert them to Valiant pilots. The spring of 1956 saw a series of high intensity trials of the Valiant's capabilities. On 2nd March 1956 a test project was approved by the RAE. It was called a dynamic loading, fatigue and vibration survey. The tests were to be carried out on a Valiant B Mk 1 aircraft,

No. WP 202. According to the paperwork completed prior to the survey the experiment would not alter the flying characteristics of the aircraft and the only alterations to the aircraft main services would be a

"power supply from aircraft to experimental equipment – approx. 50 amps required".

William Johnson, an experimental officer for RAE, was responsible for the trials on which the Valiant was engaged. He described the trials.

"Two separate vibration recording installations were fitted to the aircraft for use during the above trials. One installation was designed to record vibrations in the frequency range of approximately 40 to 500 cycles per second at approximately 20 different measuring positions distributed throughout the aircraft. The other installation was designed to do the same over a frequency range of approximately 5 to 40 cycles per second, the measuring positions being different in a number of cases, but the total number being approximately the same. A seat was fitted to the aircraft, facing forward, in the entrance well to the bomb aimers position. This position was for use of Mr Knight only while operating the experimental equipment…With the exceptions of the 35 amp master circuit breaker and most of the vibration transducers, all the equipment was positioned on the main cabin floor in front of and to the right hand of the seat provided for Mr Knight when operating the equipment. The 35 amp master circuit breaker was mounted slightly port of centre of the radio crate above the navigators table.
All this equipment was installed to operate from the 28 volt supply".

Part One: The Crash

The test flight

On 11th May 1956 Vickers Valiant B Mk 1 WP 202 took off from Farnborough on the test flight. The aircraft had been manufactured on 23rd December 1954 and had flown 153 hours. There were four people on board the plane, the pilot, Squadron Leader Kenneth Orman, the co-pilot, Flight Lieutenant Colin Donald Preece, the navigator, Flight Lieutenant Kenneth Ernest Philip Evans and a Ministry of Supply technician, Mr Alan Reginald Knight.

The long runway at Farnborough airfield was out of action due to resurfacing, so the Valiant could not take off with much fuel on board. It, therefore, flew straight to nearby Wisley where it landed to take on more fuel, which would be needed as the tests were to take several hours. The Valiant's call sign was Regent 39 and the flight call log shows that it took off from Wisley at 11.39 and started to climb. At 11.42 the pilot requested "Will you order 3 late lunches". By 12.03 it had already been established that there was a problem with the test equipment and the pilot radioed "Will be using up fuel – have a lot to burn off". Asked to repeat his message he said, "Will use up fuel awhile – our equipment is U/S". A minute later he said, "Will be staying along South Coast awhile." This was the last that was heard from the pilot before the plane crashed at 12.34.

The plane was flying east along the coast towards Southwick when the crash occurred. It hit the railway embankment just south of Croft Avenue, then exploded and disintegrated with the burnt wreckage flung almost half a mile from the point of impact in an easterly direction.

Most of the wreckage came to rest along the railway embankment and on Southwick Recreation Ground but there was also considerable damage to nearby houses. The co-pilot Flight Lieutenant Colin Preece ejected just before the crash and suffered only minor injuries but the other three crew members were all killed. The co-pilot was found in his ejector seat, which fell in an allotment patch, by local St John Ambulance man George Shuttleworth. Mr Shuttleworth said

"He was badly shaken up and had a gash on his head. I cut him loose with a knife"

Even in 1956 Southwick was quite a well built up town and the fact that no serious injuries were sustained by any civilians is remarkable. The crash occurred at 12.34 on a Friday lunch time. In the 1950s many workers still

CERTIFIED TRUE COPY 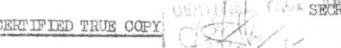 SECRET

APPENDIX " R "

WP202 VALIANT (S/L. ORMAN) 11th MAY, 1956. R/T Record.

CALL SIGN - REGENT 39.

G. M. T.

TIME	FROM	TO	R/T
1039	R39	App	Airborne Wisley 360 climbing.
	App	R39	Clear call on top
1040	R39	App	2.5 climbing /R
	R39	App	On top 3.3
	App	R39	Call level
	R39	App	Will climb right up /R
1042	R39	App	Will you order 3 late lunches. /R
1045	R39	App	What will cloud base be base in 1 hour.
	App	R39	Stand by 1 - will check.
1048	App	R39	QBB will stay 1000' for next hour.
	R39	App	OK - good show.
1103	R39	App	Will be using up fuel - have lot to burn off QNH?
	App	R39	QNH 1021 MBS Repeat last part - slightly muffled.
	R39	App	Will use up fuel awhile - our equipment is U/S.
	App	R39	R - Check steer Farnborough 020. /R.
1104	R39	App	R - Will be staying along South Coast awhile. /R (CRDF trace approx. ¾ length)
1134		CRASH	No other transmission heard.
1139½ 1140	?		Intermittent carrier only transmissions heard on 132.12 of about 5 - 6 secs duration. No trace on CRDF.

Certified that above is a true recording.

(Sgd)MR. K. W. PENDREY
Sup/Controller.

SECRET

The call log of the fatal flight

lived locally to their workplaces and would go home for lunch. Many school children would also go home at lunchtime or would be out in the playground. A senior Sussex police officer was quoted as saying

Debris along the south side of the railway embankment. The houses are in Whiterock Place

"It would appear that the pilot, knowing that he was crashing in a closely built-up area, made a desperate effort to reach the small recreation ground. At least he succeeded in that no civilians were seriously injured."

Miss F M Peck, the headmistress of Southwick Junior Girls School (The Green School), which was less than half a mile from the crash site, said

"There were more than 100 children in the playground at the time. It was a very lucky escape."

Manor Hall Road School (now Eastbrook Academy) was even closer to the site of the crash and a few pieces of wreckage actually landed in the school playground. Richard Palmer a schoolboy at the time remembers the incident well.

"I was a pupil at Manor Hall Primary School, as it was called then, adjacent to the recreation ground where the plane crashed. The crash took place during the school lunch break when we were in the playground. There was a roar of engines and I looked up to see the sky turn orange with flames (or so it seemed). There was some panic as we tried to run for safety but we were quickly ushered back to our classrooms. Miraculously, no-one on the ground was hurt - perhaps due to the skill of the pilot in finding an open space to crash the plane. A few small bits of debris landed in the playground which were circled round with chalk."

The keeper of the recreation park said

"It was a miracle no children were playing there. Another quarter of an hour and many little ones would have been out of school and romping in the park."

As it was, only five people on the ground were injured, none seriously. They were Mrs Guest, Mrs Guy, Mrs Parker, Mrs Atherfold and an unnamed man.

The accident investigation

As soon as the plane crashed the Air Ministry informed the Accidents Investigation Branch (AIB), part of the Ministry of Transport and Civil Aviation (MTCA). Two investigating officers, Mr E Newton and Mr I W Nowak then flew to Southwick to visit the scene of the crash, arriving at 17.30 that same afternoon. Their job was to secure the site and try to establish the cause of the crash. Vickers-Armstrong, the plane's manufacturers, were also very keen to know the cause of the accident and sent their own investigators to the crash site, as did the RAE, whose test plane it had been. There were, therefore, three different bodies with vested interests in the investigation into the crash. The Valiants had been operational for less than two years and so there was an urgent need to establish the cause of the crash in case other planes of that type needed to be grounded.

Mr I H Zeffert, Chief Electrical Engineer for the manufacturers, Vickers-Armstrong (Aircraft) Limited, was sent to Southwick on Saturday 12th May. He was instructed by Mr G R Edwards, Managing Director of Vickers-Armstrong to investigate whether an electrical fire had occurred on the aircraft, which could have caused the accident. A fire was suspected because a large pile of cables, panels and terminal blocks etc. were found on the ground severely burned. Also the surviving second pilot had reported that there had been some form of electrical failure. It was suspected that a short circuit may have initiated a fire in an area of the plane which contained the major part of the electrical distribution system, known as the "organ loft". The wiring in this area was concerned with the supply of 28 volts to the main system and its destruction could have caused the aircraft electrical installation to fail. However, this theory would not explain how the co-pilot had been able to report seeing fuel low pressure warning lights, as these were supplied from the 28-volt system.

The electrics on the Valiant used four 112V direct current generators, one on each of the engines, for functions requiring large amounts of power. The generators also powered a 28V DC system which was used for other systems that initiated the higher voltage system functions, and there was also a 96V backup battery. As much of the aircraft as possible was electrically driven because electrical cabling was lighter than its hydraulic equivalent and necessary for the radar. Newspapers described the Valiant as

"So complex that 38 miles of wiring are needed to take current to 85 motors and other electrical devices. With 200 instruments to check, cockpit drill takes an hour before take-off".

Mr Zeffert searched for panels and components associated with the wiring which would help to build up a picture of the state of the electrical equipment on impact. About 200 yards from the pile of wire in the recreation ground the investigators found a section of Tufnol panel and two HRC (High Rupturing Capacity) fuses, which were fitted in each of two of the main 112 volts generator systems. These were intact and unburned. Other pieces of cable with sections of main generator switch gear were found mechanically damaged but unburned. The main 112V bus bar was found complete with two large HRC fuses and various parts of other HRC distribution fuses. The bus bar was bright and new looking, had suffered no burns, and had not been subjected to any overloads. It was, however, broken and missing a section.

Accident investigators examining the burnt wiring on Southwick Recreation Ground

Mr Zeffert returned on Sunday morning to continue the search with the help of RAF crew, five RAE electrical representatives from Farnborough, other inspectors from Vickers-Armstrong and Mr Nowak from the AIB. They were asked to recover all electrical equipment possible from the scene of the

A map showing distribution of major parts of the wreckage

accident and place them together for possible identification and evidence. This took most of the day. The heap of wiring found was spread out on the recreation ground in order to identify the various sections. A survey of the whole accident area was also undertaken.

Starting from the point of impact on the railway embankment, a main generator was discovered which, though severely mechanically damaged, bore no burn marks. Within a short distance a section of the 28V distribution panel, which had housed most of the burned wiring was found, shattered and unburned. Along the south side of the railway line the investigators collected parts of the disintegrated plane and electrical components, all unburned. The missing part of the 112V bus bar, discovered in the recreation ground, was also found. The accumulator plates appeared to be in a fully charged condition and RAE were asked to try to establish whether they had been charged from the 28V system or from the 96V reserve battery, because they wanted to know whether the reserve battery was used or not during the last stages of the flight. A few parts were also collected from the north side of the railway line. The fact that none of these components showed any evidence of having been burnt led Mr Zeffert to conclude in his report that

"… it was reasonable to assume from the panels, machines and other equipment which was found damaged and unburned, that the large fire which occurred in the mass of looming found in the recreation ground was caused after the accident, by kerosene saturation and subsequent burning"

Mr Zeffert also examined all the HRC fuse carcases which could be recovered and found that those which had been physically broken all had intact fuse elements

"In all I estimate 60% of fuse bodies or intact fuses were recovered of those normally fitted to the 112V bus bar. These showed no sign of electrical overload. Particularly, continuity was established on the main flap fuse and one main chassis fuse. Subsequently in two main generator fuses continuity was established by RAE. This evidence can be construed to indicate that the 112V system had failed entirely and not by a succession of individual circuit failures."

Mr Zeffert's report was submitted to the subsequent RAF Court of Inquiry.

Another line of inquiry for the investigators related to two nickel plated brass clips from the voltage regulator. It had been found previously when servicing another Valiant, WP 203, that some of the clips on the voltage regulator were broken. If these clips were to become loose in a certain way the voltage regulation could become affected and some, if not all, of the generators thrown off the line. However, Mr Ripley, the Head of RAE Accidents Investigation Section (Structures Department) later reported

"A search was therefore made among the pieces of WP 202 to see whether a similar defect had occurred and whether it might conceivably have been a contributory cause to the electrical failure of the aircraft. Insufficient parts have been found in the wreckage to give a conclusive story, but I think it is rather an unlikely possibility"

The Court of Inquiry

The RAF ordered a Court of Inquiry for the purpose of

(a) *determining the cause of an accident to Valiant B.1 WP 202, near Shoreham, Sussex on 11th May, 1956, resulting in the deaths of Sqn.Ldr. K. Orman (56842), Flt. Lt. K.E.P. Evans (157970) and Mr A.R. Knight*

(b) *allocating responsibility*

(c) *recording damage to civilian property*

(d) *establishing that all members of the crew were on duty at the time of the accident*

(e) *making recommendations, if any.*

(f) *evidence to be taken on oath.*

The Court assembled on 13th May at RAE Farnborough by order of Air Commodore J M Cohu CBE, Air Officer Commanding, No. 61 group.

The Court was comprised of Wing Commander H J Cundall from RAF Wittering, the president of the Court, and Flight Lieutenant V J Glanville from RAF Boscombe Down. Mr E L Ripley OBE, the Head of RAE Accidents Investigation Section (Structures Department) and Squadron Leader R T Potgieter of HQ Bomber Command were also in attendance. The Court convened on the morning of Sunday 13th May and flew to Shoreham Airport. After visiting Shoreham Police Station, to arrange for the interviews of civilian witnesses, they went to Southwick Recreation Ground to visit the scene of the accident to survey the wreckage. They met the Air Investigation Branch representatives and a number of other investigating specialists.

They agreed with the Air Investigation Branch representatives that removal of the wreckage could now be authorised. The Court spent the next four and a half days interviewing witnesses and discussing with experts. On Tuesday afternoon they flew to Shoreham again to examine the civilian witness statements. They also took the evidence of Sergeant Frank Bulpeck, who was the day duty sergeant at Shoreham-By-Sea police station on 11th May and who had received a 999 call by telephone at 12.37 to the effect that an aircraft had crashed at Southwick. The Court then visited the accident scene again.

In total six witnesses were interviewed at Shoreham by Sergeant Bulpeck and other local policemen and sixteen at Farnborough by the Court.

Wreckage strewn across Southwick Recreation Ground. You can see the Westland Whirlwind helicopter belonging to the accident investigators

The first witness was the co-pilot Flight Lieutenant Colin Preece who gave evidence from 9.30 to 17.00 on Monday and for a further hour on Tuesday morning. He was also recalled again briefly on Thursday 17th May. He told the inquiry that after taking off from Wisley, having refuelled with 4,000 gallons, they climbed to 11,000 feet to carry out the first test.

"I don't know when Mr Knight switched on his test equipment but a short time after we reached 11,000 feet he reported that power was not getting through to his equipment. He said a breaker kept popping out. It was my impression that Mr Knight had already made several attempts to get his equipment working but that each time the breaker popped out. After a little discussion Mr Knight asked the Captain if he could hold the breaker in to see if that would do any good. S/L Orman agreed and Mr Knight tried this without success. After about a minute he said he could still get no power to his camera. The Captain asked Mr Knight to confirm that there was no hope of his equipment becoming serviceable. Mr Knight said the equipment was quite U/S and the Captain then called Farnborough, told them the equipment was unserviceable and said he was descending to burn off fuel"

The weather conditions that day were cloudy but during the early part of the flight the captain had noticed areas clear of cloud over the South Coast. So it was decided to head southerly and when they noticed a gap in the cloud to port they turned easterly and headed down through the gap, levelling out at approximately 1,000 feet about one mile out to sea from Selsey Bill. Flight

Lieutenant Preece was flying the plane at this point. The captain decided they should stay at this height and at a speed of 280 to 300 knots.

"There was a good deal of low cloud in the vicinity. It was mostly over the land and the base was below the height at which we were flying. We made two return journeys in this area, turning at each end towards the sea."

In order to extend its flying range the Valiant had additional external fuel tanks fitted to the underside of the wings. During the flying backwards and forwards it became necessary to change the fuel feed from the fuselage to the wing tanks. The Captain took over the controls of the aircraft so that the co-pilot could change the fuel feed and read the fuel content gauges. The fuel would need to be managed from the different tanks to keep the plane balanced. The fuel cycling came around approximately every seven minutes. After the second run to Shoreham the aircraft turned again at Selsey Bill and the Navigator, Flight Lieutenant Evans, asked for the next fuel cycle. Flight Lieutenant Preece said

"I switched on the fuselage tanks and switched off all the wing tanks and almost immediately the two starboard low pressure warning lights came on, i.e. the two lights in front of me….I drew the captains attention to the lights and he immediately switched the wing tanks on. At this time both lamps flickered out and immediately came on again."

The aircraft was now flying parallel with the coast on an easterly heading. The captain announced that the tail trim had gone and appeared to put the aircraft into a very slight climb. He then said "we're in manual" and asked the co-pilot to get on to the controls with him. The plane climbed to about 2,000 feet and entered thin cloud. The captain called up Farnborough and said that they were in trouble, but Flight Lieutenant Preece did not recall Farnborough's reply and it appears that Farnborough did not receive the message. At this stage the navigator reported that the generators and invertors had failed.

"From the time that the Captain said we were in manual control he repeatedly told me to pull. This we both did and I placed my left foot upon the instrument panel to get more purchase. The right foot cannot, of course, be used for this purpose because of obstructions. In my opinion our combined efforts had little or no effect in changing the attitude of the aeroplane. I don't remember observing the airspeed indicator during this period but it is my belief that our speed did not decrease appreciably from the figure of 280 to 300 knots at which we had been flying….We both tried hard to apply Starboard Aileron but without effect. At about this point we cleared the thin cloud we had been in and by a visual reference it was clear that we were now descending. As far as I was concerned the ailerons and elevators were immoveable, the ailerons being as near as I could judge neutral and the stick in normal position for the elevators. Up to this time I had imagined that our efforts on the stick had produced the climb but I now think that the climb was initiated by the Captain before we reverted to manual.

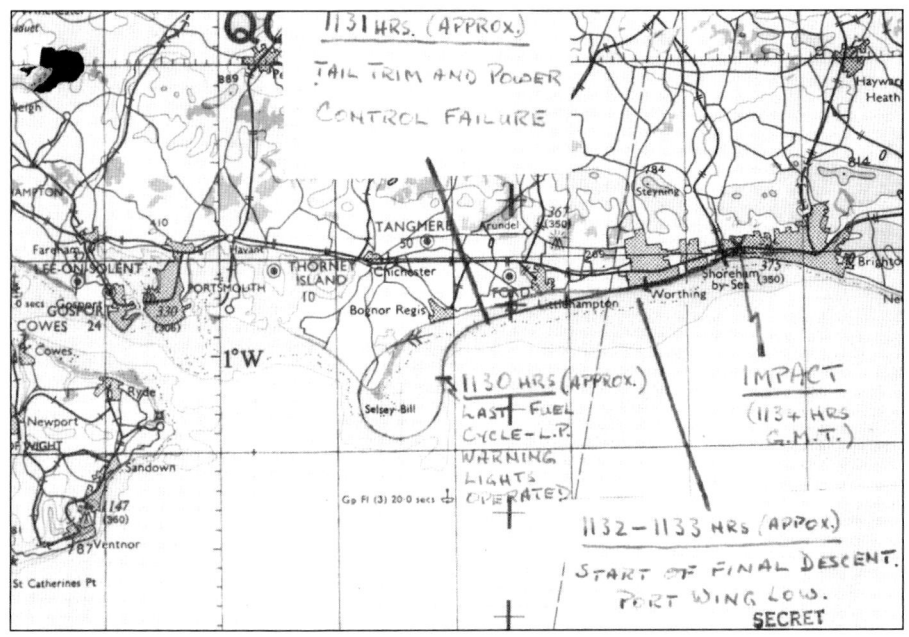

A map showing the final flight path of Valiant WP 202 as it flew from Shoreham to Selsey then back towards Southwick

After descending for a little while the captain said "get out". I think this was at about 1,500 feet because when I looked at the altimeter shortly afterwards we were passing through 1,000 feet. There was some cloud still below us but through a gap I saw a town. I had heard nothing from the crew in the back recently and I told the Captain that I was blowing the hood. I heard no reply from him. The hood went and it was quite comfortable in the cockpit. I think our speed at this time would be about 320 knots, and we were in a turning descent to port, nose down 5 to 10° approximately.

I felt for the blind handle with both hands but appeared to be unable to reach it. Eventually I got it with my right hand. I pulled but it did not fire immediately but with a further and harder pull the seat fired.

From this time I was somewhat disorientated and remember nothing clearly until I found myself sitting in the local railway station where I had been taken for first aid attention".

Flight Lieutenant Preece also gave evidence to the inquest which was held in Shoreham Town Hall on 13th June 1956. He said, once the test equipment was found to be unserviceable

"It was decided to abandon the sortie and return to Farnborough. We were overweight for landing and it was necessary to fly around to use up some of the fuel. The pilot decided to fly at 1,000 ft as the fuel consumption is greater at lower altitudes. ...On the second turn round Selsey we had just completed the turn and headed for the coast when Squadron Leader Orman said we had lost the use of the variable incidence tail trimmer. We went into manual control, which means we lost the power assistance to the flight controls, and the forces you have to apply to control the aircraft are very much increased.... At 1,500 ft Squadron Leader Orman gave the order to get out over the intercom. This applied to all on board. Flight Lieutenant Evans and Mr Knight were wearing earphones and we had all been chatting previously... Evans and Knight had no ejector seats but had parachutes and there was a door in the left-hand side of the plane through which they had to go out."

In answer to a question Flight Lieutenant Preece said he and Squadron Leader Orman were doing all they could to keep the plane climbing before the crash.

"I am quite sure that he stayed in the plane to let us all get out".

Expert witnesses

The fact that the Valiant had been modified in order to carry out the vibration tests was obviously a major focus of the RAF Inquiry. Had the alterations to the aeroplane caused it to crash? The initial paperwork, Special Instrumentation Forms P1 and P2, which were completed in March stated that the experiment would not alter the flying characteristics of the aircraft. The only alterations made to the aircraft main services would be a power supply from the aircraft to the equipment, requiring approximately 50 amps. In his witness statement Mr Norman Carey, the RAE mechanic who carried out the modifications explained that he had

"tapped off a 28 volts supply from a heavy-duty terminal block (B2) situated behind panel G which fed in a 70 amp cable from an 80 HRC fuse on panel Z. This seemed a very suitable supply point because I estimated that the other loads on this fuse did not exceed 20 amps."

These electrical alterations were actually made to meet the needs of two separate trials in the aircraft's programme. The Valiant flew on a different trial for several weeks before Mr Johnson's vibration survey equipment was installed, replacing the earlier trials equipment. When the vibration survey equipment was installed it was found that it took more current than initially indicated and it was necessary to step up the 12 amp cable to 24 and to substitute a 45 amp master circuit breaker for the 35 amp one initially specified.

"An ammeter was placed in the circuit and on full load read 32 amps. This was still within very safe limits for the HRC fuse chosen. The whole installation was

subsequently passed by inspection and it operated in the air on two or three flights during the following week or so. On the days when the Valiant did not fly the equipment was run for half an hour at Mr Johnsons request."

Mr Thomas Thompson, Technical Class Grade 2 Aircraft Inspector was responsible for examining and clearing the completed installation of Mr Johnson's trial equipment. This was completed as required by the relevant forms P1 and P2.

"It was run and checked and the cables from the 35 amp circuit breaker which were in the 12 amp Pren were warm. Mr Johnson was contacted and in discussion with him in the aircraft it was agreed between us to substitute 24 amp cable for the 12 amp cable and to put in a 45 amp circuit breaker to replace the existing 35 amp one. We had at this stage made a check to find out what current was being taken by the test equipment and found this to be about 11 amps instead of the 10 amps shown on the P2 drawing. An ammeter was placed in the circuit and as a result of these tests I was informed that the combined current of the three circuits was 32 amps. The final inspection with the 24 amp cable and the 45 amp circuit breaker fitted was made sometime in the week preceding 7th May 1956. It was on the day of the inspection that Mr Johnson did his functional tests before I cleared the installation for flight."

Mr Thompson then told the Court that he could find no entry on the Form 700 paperwork to cover this work. He was, however, quite certain that he properly checked and was satisfied with the installation. A Form 700 recorded all servicing, modifications, repairs and refuelling carried out on an aircraft. It had to be signed by the crew prior to flight. To enable any servicing to be done away from base to be recorded, a second Form 700, marked in red "Travelling Copy" was carried with the aircraft and the details contained in the copy were transferred to the original form on return.

Mr Thompson also stated that

"The decision to change the cables and circuit breaker contrary to the items specified in Form P2 was regarded as a safety measure but not as a major alteration to the installation. Due to the limitations of the Forms P1 and P2 submitted for this installation, these forms being typical of what we get to work from, the changes which we made were quite small compared with the amount of interpretation which we must make on the Forms. The forms in this case were in fact better than some we have had. Even so they leave the physical layout of the boxes and wiring in the aircraft and also the power feed pick up point quite unspecified. The discussion with Mr Johnson on changing the installation as drawn was quite informal but I personally was quite satisfied that what we were doing was sound".

Mr Johnson when asked by the Court did not recollect this discussion with Mr Thompson. He said

"From discussions since the accident I have been led to understand that a 45 amp circuit breaker and other changes in the weight of power supplies wiring were actually incorporated into the installation in the aircraft instead of the items specified on Form P2 Sheet 1. I was aware earlier that the weight of wire between the 35 amp and 15 amp circuit breakers had been increased in order to avoid excessive voltage drop. This had been done on another aircraft, Valiant WP 214, in almost identical circumstances. As regards the change of circuit breaker from 35 amp to 45 amp I do not recall ever having discussed this matter with anybody before the accident. I would not necessarily expect to have been consulted over such a change but in my opinion the authority for such change should have been given by the responsible authority in the electrical department who had originally approved Form P2."

Who that responsible authority was remains a mystery as Form P2 was not actually signed.

Valiant WP 202's previous flight

On 10th May, the day before the crash, Mr George Burton, another Flight Observer with the RAE, flew in the Valiant and used the test equipment which Mr Knight went up the following day to use. He was scheduled to take recordings of take-off and landing.

"On entering the aircraft I switched on the 3 fifteen amp circuit breakers and the switch, all of which control amplifiers, recorder and calibrating equipment. In fact this was all the equipment installed for this particular job. I was sitting in the observer's position port side at the back and when the engines started I switched in the 35 amp circuit breaker (which I now know was in fact a 45 amp one). All the equipment then appeared to function correctly.

As we were about to take off I pressed the recorder remote control button at the observers position (port side back), and watched the recorder to see whether the red light came on which indicates by flashing, (once every foot), that the film is traversing through the recorder. Another record was taken as we were about to unstick. On neither occasion did the red light flash. I did not examine the recorder as we were landing at Wisley in a very short time. I took records of the approach and landing at Wisley and again had no red lights. I did not suspect that the recorder might not be working as it was not unusual for the red light not to come on".

As on the following day the Valiant had flown straight from Farnborough to Wisley to refuel. There was a delay at Wisley, caused by tyre failure, and it was decided to postpone the tests until the following day and return straight to Farnborough. When the aircraft took off from Wisley to return to Farnborough Mr Burton again checked that all his equipment was functioning properly.

"I again operated the remote control to take records on take off and landing and once again there was no indication on the red lights that the film was traversing in the recorder. As soon as we landed I opened the recorder to take out the used film and found that it was crinkled around the rollers in an unusual way. I removed the film and developed it later and found that it had not moved in the recorder during the whole of these two flights.

The next morning Mr Knight decided to fly on these tests and I took him over to the aircraft and told him of the difficulty I had had with the recorder. I suggested that he should be extra careful in loading the film".

Mr Basil Maries, an Aircraft Inspector from RAE, Farnborough, told the Inquiry that he had gone to Wisley on 11th May to receive Valiant WP 202 and to supervise its refuelling and between-flight inspection and to clear it for its next flight.

"When it landed I spoke to each member of the crew and they reported no defects. I fully inspected the aircraft and can confirm that the total fuel load after refuelling was 4008 gallons. During my inspection the bomb doors were not opened for security reasons. I cleared the aircraft for flight at 11.30 and handed the travelling copy of the F.700 to the captain. Valiant WP 202 had the original trials installation completed on 5th March 1956 and I was responsible for its inspection and clearance. Having satisfied myself of its sound workmanship and proved by test that it functioned I cleared the installation."

Mr Cyril Berens, Chief Engineer Airfield, RAE, MOS, Farnborough testified that he had examined the normal servicing documents of Valiant WP 202 and found them to be all correct. He also confirmed that the modifications for the test complied with the requirements as advised by the RTO for Valiant aircraft of the CA fleet.

Flight Lieutenant Ernest Pennie, GD Pilot of the RAE Experimental Flying Department presented to the Court details of the weather during the flight, the weight and condition of the aircraft and the personal particulars of all the crew members. Squadron Leader Orman was 33 years old. He was the pilot, sitting in the left cockpit seat. He had a total of 3,074 flying hours, 147 of those on Valiants. His last flying training assessment had been average. Flight Lieutenant Colin Preece was the second pilot, sitting in the right cockpit seat. He had 1,731 flying hours, 30 of them on Valiants. Flight Lieutenant Evans was the navigator sitting in the navigator's cabin. He had 3,321 flying hours, 47 of them on Valiants. Mr A Knight was the Ministry of Supply flight observer, also seated in the navigator's cabin. No flying hours were available, but he was described as very experienced.

Flight Lieutenant Evans

In his witness statement Wing Commander John Finch, Wing Commander Flying, Farnborough also gave an account of the crew.

"Squadron Leader Orman was one of the most experienced Valiant pilots on the unit. He was in charge of the V bomber flight and having flown with him frequently in recent months, I am more than normally confident in my assessment of his ability. He was an above the average test pilot in this type of work. The co-pilot is an above the average pilot who was fully competent to fly as co-pilot. The navigator had over 3,000 hours flying and had flown in the Valiant frequently in recent weeks. Mr Knight was a very experienced Flight Observer and was recognised as being exceptionally able".

Wing Commander Finch then addressed the training methods at Farnborough which had been under scrutiny.

"As regards the conversion training, the type of work here calls for unconventional methods of crew member training. The smaller numbers involved allows a greater degree of individual treatment. The work of the unit demands much more concentrated attention to the technical aspect of flying at all times and it is essential that flexibility be retained to fly different types for purposes of comparison and other reasons.... The small number of crews involved allows the flexibility in crewing which the work at RAE requires. Our standard crew is 3 regular members, based on not carrying more crew than is essential. The two spare seats may be partly or fully occupied by essential technical observers or additional crew members for special purposes. Our drills and crew responsibilities have been specifically designed to suit this arrangement and I am satisfied that they are completely adequate."

Wing Commander Finch was asked about the captain's decision to fly the aircraft at low altitude.

"Whilst I agree that the Captain's airmanship while flying the aircraft at 1,000 feet in the weather conditions prevailing is open to question special instructions associated with the test in hand precluded flying over built up areas. As this pilot's airmanship has always been good I believe that he was anxious to keep visual to avoid flying over towns".

The co-pilot Flight Lieutenant Preece had already told the Court that he flew on at least one other occasion with Squadron Leader Orman when it became necessary to use up surplus fuel.

"On that occasion he adopted a similar pattern for this purpose at much the same height and in much the same area".

Civilian witnesses

The civilian witnesses did not have to attend the Court in Farnborough but were interviewed by the local Shoreham police. They were all asked to describe what they saw. In particular, the Court wanted to know how the plane was flying, how high it was, whether they saw anything fall from the plane and did they see any fire onboard the plane.

Walter Hancorn, of The Gardens, a general foreman at Brighton B Power Station, was on his way home from the power station and about to cross the lock gates when he heard a plane approach and saw it coming down out of the mist.

"It was flying quite low and gradually losing height. The left wing was lower than the other at something like 50° and the machine was banking. After passing me it seemed to gain a little height and I watched it over the houses. The next thing was the explosion. My reaction was of surprise at the crash. As the plane passed over me it was alarmingly low but I could see nothing wrong the machine and it was intact. There was no sign of fire.

I can't say anything about the plane's engines – there was plenty of noise but so far as I know it was just the noise a jet engine makes.

It was in my view until it passed over the row of houses. It came in from the south west and kept a straight course, passed over me at the lock gate and I am sure there was no fire visible.

I saw nothing come from the machine."

Retired Squadron Leader Cyril Streeter, of Norfolk Terrace, was standing in his garden facing the sea.

A map showing the position of the civilian witnesses to the Court of Inquiry

"when I noticed a Valiant Jet Bomber coming along the sea edge from the direction of Worthing -W -East.

It was about 700/1000 feet up. I noticed particularly that the aircraft looked and appeared to be flying slightly left wing low. She appeared to be keeping a very straight course. I followed the machine with my eyes until it disappeared in the region of the Electricity Power Station. It was rather misty at the time. I am positive that, from my view, there was no fire at the time the machine passed, but very slight smoke appeared to be coming from the rear of the tail pipe. By the sound of the motors they appeared quite normal. I have 38 years with the RAF and am now a retired officer. I clearly recognised the aircraft as a Valiant Jet Bomber and was very surprised to learn, within a few minutes, that it had crashed."

Police Constable Ivo Setterfield was in the area of Kings Crescent on Shoreham Beach when he heard the sound of a jet aircraft.

"I looked up and towards the sea and saw an aircraft that I identified as a Vickers Valiant.

It seemed to me that, although it was low, it was alright and apart from the fact that the left wing was low it flew in an easterly direction. I lost sight of the aircraft and continued with what I was doing.

I was later informed by Ex Squadron Leader Streeter that this plane had crashed and later mentioned to PS 15 Bulbeck that I had seen the aircraft in question."

Ernest Burstow, of Lower Bevendean, Brighton, was an excavator driver at Walter Llewelyn at the Peter Linds Site, Middle Pier, adjoining the lighthouse.

"I was standing with my works foreman, Mr Henry Bathie, on the site facing west. We heard a bang, looked up and saw a large jet aircraft with swept back wings coming out of the mist losing altitude. Having served in the Royal Air Force for nearly seven years and with some 12 hours flying I watched the flight of this aircraft. When it came out of the mist it was flying on a direct course from the direction of the Isle of Wight going slightly in land. It was flying port wing low at about 45°. The cockpit cover (escape hatch) dropped about 15 feet west of the lifeboat station in the river. The plane passed right over us and was so low that the driver of our derrick with a 120 foot jib jumped down for safety. We watched it lose altitude and as it passed over the main coast road in Southwick there was another bang and we saw a parachute partly open up and disappear behind the houses in Southwick. Almost immediately there was another report as the plane crashed. When we saw it, from my experience the plane was intact. I would be willing to attend a Court of Enquiry if called upon to do so. There was no fire."

Lawrence Hubbard, of Albion Street, Southwick, was a crane driver operating the east crane at Tuberville Wharf. He was in his cab approximately 50 feet above ground level. He had just finished work and was facing out to sea.

"I heard a jet approaching from the west, there was a very low mist, I saw a jet which I knew to be a Valiant bomber. As I saw it come over the Old Fort, west of the harbour entrance I estimate its height about 300 feet. It was on an even keel and did not appear to be in any trouble. It was definitely not flying at full throttle.

The plane flew on a perfectly straight course and was in true flight, the plane came from the harbour entrance practically dead over my crane and passed slightly to the north of the Methodist Church in Albion St. where I saw the member of the crew ejected from the plane. That was the first time I realised it was in trouble.

I still followed the plane and saw it strike the railway lines which I thought to be near the recreation field. It struck the line and immediately there was a terrific ball of flame, I then lost sight of the plane.

I followed the plane from the time it appeared from the sea to the time it struck the bank. Nothing fell off the plane, there was no sign of fire. The plane appeared to me to be in perfect condition. It was not diving but was in a gentle glide. It did not vary its course a fraction at any time."

Alexander Davison, of 18 Buci Crescent, Shoreham, was working in the office of Central Garage, Albion Street, when he heard the noise of a low flying plane.

"The noise gave me the impression that the engines may have been turned off and the machine was more or less coasting along when I looked up. There was no flame or smoke that I could see and although it's difficult to be accurate I would estimate its height at

about 40/80 feet. I saw something fly out of the plane when it first came into view to the south west of the office. As the plane passed over I saw it was losing height, the nose being down slightly. The machine travelled S/W – N/E straight over my yard and I saw that it was inching towards the north in an arc. So far as I could see the wings were level with one another. There was no fire. I walked across the yard to watch the plane out of sight and saw that there was no fire externally. I've since heard that the plane passed over "like a ball of fire" but this is not so in my case. I heard the explosion very shortly afterwards and I had no doubt what had happened. I went to the scene to see what I could do. I handed in a glove that fell out of the plane as it passed over my yard. The plane was travelling very slowly as it passed over."

Evidence of MOT Accidents Investigation Branch and RAE Accidents Investigation Section

The most comprehensive account of the crash impact and damage caused was given by Mr Wladyslaw Nowak, Accidents Investigation Branch, Ministry of Transport and Civil Aviation. He presented his report to the Court.

"I am the Investigating Officer, on the staff of the Chief Inspector of Accidents.

I first visited the scene of the accident to Valiant B1. WP 202 at about 1730 hrs on 11.5.56, in the company of the Chief Investigating Officer AIB (Mr E. Newton) having been called in to assist the Inquiry by D.F.S. Air Ministry.

The crater at the point of impact

Examination showed that the aircraft had first struck the south embankment of the railway close to Southwick Station. This impact had been made with the aircraft whilst it was in a shallow dive at a high speed and almost laterally level, on a heading of about 80° mag. The violent impact disrupted the rail track and electric power cables, and made a crater in the embankment about 90 ft. x 30 ft. x 8 ft. The aircraft completely disintegrated following this impact and wreckage was flung forward for about 700 yards (see wreckage plot). A flash fire developed probably from compression ignition of fuel tanks. Considerable damage to civilian dwellings, gardens and council recreation grounds was caused by flying debris. My examination of all the wreckage in the field revealed no evidence of a sustained pre-crash fire. The burning, such as it was, of most of the wreckage was not severe, and was typical of small quantities of fuel adhering to the fragments. Out of 17 fire extinguisher bottle heads recovered, two appeared to have operated. Further detailed investigation will be made into this aspect.

Clockwise from top right: photos of engine combustion chamber, engine compressor, turbine, jet pipe

All four engines, which were found about 600 yards from the first impact, showed clear evidence that they had been rotating when the accident occurred. There was no evidence to suggest pre-crash mechanical failure or fire in the air at the engine installation.

All flying controls were severely damaged but the condition of the actuators and screw jacks suggested that the aircraft configuration and trim at the moment of impact was as follows: -

Starboard:	Aileron trim tab	:	.350" up i.e. port bank
	Rudder trim tab	:	Neutral
	Elevator trim tab	:	1 ½ ° up
	Tailplane incidence	:	+ 1° 20'
	Air brakes	:	Out
	Flaps	:	Up
	Undercarriage	:	Up

Note: The full travel of the aileron trim tab from neutral is .800"

The remains of the extensively damaged power controls, when examined, precluded any immediate useful evidence. These will, however, be subjected to detailed expert examination. There is no immediate evidence of pre-impact structural failure of the airframe or control surfaces but special attention will be paid to the controls and control surfaces at the RAE.

The Captain's safety harness was extensively damaged in the crash. Inspection of the release box and strap lugs, however, indicate that he was strapped in when the aircraft struck the ground. There was no evidence to suggest the other two occupants were strapped in. From the two parachute release boxes recovered only one (unidentified) showed marks suggesting that the parachute harness was fastened. Due to lack of evidence on the harness and the fact that, so far, I have not been able to establish whether or not the crew escape door had been jettisoned, I am unable to say how far the occupants had progressed with their escape drill.

Harness and parachute release boxes

So far as the investigation has progressed no defect or failure in the electrical or flying control system has been found which may have caused or contributed to this accident. However, owing to the nature of the accident it is recommended that the wreckage be transported to the RAE Farnborough where further detailed inspection can be made in collaboration with the electrical specialists of the RAE and Vickers Armstrong (Aviation) Ltd."

A starboard elevator and a rudder with trim

The final witness to give evidence to the Court was Mr Eric Ripley OBE Head of RAE Accidents Investigation Section (Structures Department) Farnborough.

"On the day of the accident I was at Boscombe Down and was immediately flown to Shoreham. I commenced examination of the wreckage together with representatives of the Accidents Investigation Branch (MTCA) and experts from the RAE and the firm (Vickers). I now produce a local plan showing the distribution of the wreckage at the site. When the court assembled on 13th May 1956 I joined them in attendance as requested in the convening signal and outlined to them the work that had already been done. Later in the day I visited the scene of the accident with the court, and the President cleared the wreckage for return to RAE Farnborough for further investigation. By this time evidence was mounting that the electrical system of the aircraft was suspect and particular efforts were made to locate as many components as possible of the electrical system amongst the debris. The examination of these components and of the electrical installation of the aircraft generally was then continued at very high priority by both RAE and the firm.

I have been with the court throughout the majority of its sittings and have seen all the evidence given before it and I have also been in close touch with the whole work of this accident in the RAE.

In addition Vickers Armstrong have kept me informed of the work they are doing and I have supplied them with relevant information on the circumstances of the accident to guide them in this work.

The preliminary results of all this work suggests that a single fault in any one of several places in the electrical installation can jeopardise the safety of the aircraft.

Finally I here produce a transcript of all messages to and from Valiant WP 202 as recorded by RAE Air Traffic Control."

Valiants grounded

On the fourth day of the Inquiry a signal was sent by the President of the Court, Wing Commander Cundall, to the Air Ministry advocating Valiant restrictions. The signal reads as follows

"FROM PRESIDENT, COURT OF INQUIRY ACCIDENT VALLIANT WP.202(.) IMMEDIATE REPORT UNDER A.M.O. A.362/55 PARA. 30 FOLLOWS(.) PARA 2 STRONG EVIDENCE SO FAR OBTAINED INDICATES COMPLETE FAILURE OF 112 VOLT POWER SUPPLIES UNDER FOLLOWING BRIEF CONDITIONS:- (A) HEIGHT 1000 FEET IN VISUAL FLIGHT(.) (B) SPEED 280 TO 300 KTS IAS(.) (C) ATTITUDE STRAIGHT AND LEVEL, PROBABLY WITH SLIGHT NOSE-UP TRIM(.) PARA 3 KNOWING SOMETHING OF THE CONTROL FORCES DEMANDED WITH THE VALIANT IN MANUAL GRAVE DOUBT ARISES WHETHER COMBINED EFFORTS OF BOTH PILOTS ON CONTROLS FROM THAT POINT ONWARDS RESULTED IN ANY NOTICABLE CHANGE OF AIRCRAFT'S FLIGHT PATH BEFORE IMPACT APPROXIMATELY TWO TO THREE MINUTES LATER(.) DIVE BRAKES WERE EXTENDED THROUGHOUT THE INCIDENT(.) POWER WAS REDUCED(.) IT IS IMPROBABLE THAT SPEED UP TO POINT OF IMPACT EVER DECREASED BELOW 250 KTS OR INCREASED BEYOND 320 KTS(.) PARA 4 THERE IS NO (R) NO EVIDENCE SO FAR THAT SPECIAL TRIALS EQUIPMENT FITTED TO THIS AIRCRAFT HAD ANY DIRECT BEARING ON ACCIDENT(.) EXPERT TECHNICAL ADVICE DISCUSSED BUT NOT YET FORMALLY RECORDED ALREADY INDICATES EXISTENCE OF SEVERAL SINGLE POSSIBLE CAUSES OF COMPLETE FAILURE OF THIS NATURE IN STANDARD VALIANT ELECTRICAL SYSTEM(.) PARA 5 POWER FAILURE OF THIS NATURE RESULTS IN IMMEDIATE FAILURE OF ALL POWER CONTROLS, VARIABLE INCIDENCE TAIL PLANE ACTUATOR, ALL RADAR AND OTHER IMPORTANT SYSTEMS(.) IN ADDITION 28 VOLT SUPPLIES BECOME LIMITED TO CAPACITY REMAINING IN BATTERY(.) PARA 6 IT IS PROBABLE THAT THIS ACCIDENT HIGHLIGHTS A CONDITION WHICH, IN SPITE OF MANY OTHER SAFETY MEASURES, HAS NOT BEFORE

BEEN FULLY ASSESSED.   URGENT ATTENTION IS THEREFORE
COMMENDED TO: (A) COMPLETE EXAMINATION OF VALIANT
ELECTRICAL SYSTEM WITH VIEW TO FINDING AND REDUCING
TO ACCEPTABLE STANDARDS ALL POSSIBLE CAUSES OF
SUCH FAILURE(.)   (B)   FURTHER FLYING TESTS TO
DETERMINE ACCEPTABLE LIMITATIONS FOR AN EMERGENCY
OF THIS NATURE FROM THE POINT OF VIEW OF MANAGEABLE
CONTROL LOADS WHEN ELECTRICAL TRIMING DEVICES ARE
NO LONGER OPERABLE(.)   PARA 7   PENDING COMPLETION
OF WORK REQUIRED BY PARA 6 IMMEDIATE CONSIDERATION
IS DEMANDED OF THE FOLLOWING:-   (A)   IMPOSITION OF
SEVERE RESTRICTIONS ON HIGH SPEED FLYING AT LOW
ALTITUDES SO THAT CONTROL CAN BE MAINTAINED ON
EMERGENCY REVERSION TO MANUAL(.)   AT THE PRESENT
LIMIT OF 360   (R)   360 KTS IT IS THOUGHT TO BE
IMPOSSIBLE TO MANOEUVRE THE AIRCRAFT WHEN COMPLETE
FAILURE OF ELECTRICAL POWER SUPPLY CAUSES REVERSION
TO MANUAL(.)   IF THERE IS INSUFFICIENT KNOWLEDGE TO
DETERMINE ACCEPTABLE LIMITS IN THIS CONDITION THE
AIRCRAFT SHOULD BE GROUNDED(.)   (B)   RESTRICTIONS
ON OPERATING WEATHER MINIMA NECESSARY AS LOSS
OF ELECTRICS REMOVES NAVIGATIONAL AIDS(.)   (C)
RESTRICTION OF AIRCRAFT TO MODERATE ATTITUDES AT LOW
ALTITUDES TO REDUCE THE DEMAND FOR LARGE ATTITUDE
CHANGES SHOULD REVERSION TO MANUAL OCCUR(.)"

On Thursday 17th May the Air Ministry issued a statement, reported in, amongst other papers, the Coventry Evening Telegraph.

"Pending inquiries into last week's accident, Bomber Command Valiants are not flying, but no formal Air Ministry instruction to ground them has been issued."

The paper went on to report

"The Press Association understands that a decision to ground an aircraft has to be authorised by the Chief of the Air Staff. The "no flying" decision has been made by the Air Officer Commanding-in-Chief, Bomber Command."

The Belfast News-Letter reported a statement from the plane manufacturers, Vickers-Armstrong.

"It appears possible that last week's accident could have been caused by an electrical failure of a rare kind and which could only happen in an unusual and complicated set of

circumstances. Modifications to safeguard against this would be relatively quick to install. The matter is being actively pursued."

Court findings

On Friday 18th May after sitting for five and a half days the Court of Inquiry decided that, rather than waiting for every avenue of inquiry into the cause of the crash to be investigated, it was important for them to make their findings known, so that any recommendations could be implemented immediately. They spent the whole of Friday afternoon considering the evidence and reaching their conclusions.

They found that: -

(a) *The accident was caused by rapid failure without previous warning of the 112 volt power supply. When the tail trim and power controls failed the aircraft was flying straight and level with probably slight nose-up trim (as may well have been applied in the preceding turn). The speed was 280-300 knts and at this speed it remained beyond effective control, though the combined efforts of both pilots were applied and normal measures to reduce speed were taken without marked effect.*

(b) *This accident highlights a condition which, in spite of many other safety measures built into the Valiant, has never before been fully assessed. Preliminary results of wide spread and intensive specialist investigation show that a single fault in any one of several places in the standard Valiant's electrical installation can jeopardise the safety of the aircraft.*

(c) *Though the specialist test equipment is still being investigated there is no proof that it contributed to the power supply failure. At the most it may have touched a weak feature in the Valiant's normal electrical system.*

(d) *The system of defining special test installations for aircraft appears inadequate and the records on Form 700 in this case were not complete.*

(e) *There is no evidence of fire in the air but the Valiant's fire warning system is not comprehensive or adequate.*

(f) *The crew were all on duty and the flight was properly authorised.*

(g) *The injury to civilians and damage to property was miraculously small considering the circumstances.*

(h) *In the final stages of the Court's deliberations it has become apparent that it could more usefully serve by speedily concluding its evidence and making known the facts and urgent recommendations than by following through the highly technical enquiries which are now in progress. This it decided to do.*

(i) The conversion training given to Valiant crews at Farnborough is unorthodox. This point was the subject of much consideration and undoubtedly special circumstances obtain, particularly governing the number of fully trained crew carried on normal sorties. It is evident that the authorities in charge of these matters at Farnborough are very aware of their importance but it seems possible that fuller advantage might profitably be taken of the training facilities available and the methods used in the Royal Air Force. It is not suggested that inadequate crew training contributed directly in any way to this particular accident. The Court wish to make this clear.

(j) The airmanship displayed by the captain in flying at 1,000 ft to use up fuel in weather conditions which imposed some limitations has been questioned. The Court is of the opinion that this was a borderline case in view of the special trial conditions imposed and sees no useful purpose in labouring it further.

Recommendations

The Court has made preliminary recommendations: -

(a) The Valiant electrical system requires urgent and complete expert examination to discover and reduce to acceptable standards all possible causes of power failure that can so easily jeopardise the aircrafts' safety. (What precisely caused this accident appears to be of secondary importance to this wider issue).

(b) The manageable control forces on sudden and unexpected reversion to manual control without subsequent use of electrical services must be determined by practical tests unless such a possibility can be entirely removed.

(c) The imposition of severe restrictions on high speed flying at low altitudes so that control can be maintained on emergency revision to manual is essential pending the action being completed on the recommendations at (a) and (b). If there is insufficient knowledge to determine acceptable limits in this condition the aircraft should be grounded.

(d) Operating weather minima for Valiant aircraft should be reviewed taking into account the possible loss of navigation aids due to electrical failure.

Further Recommendations

(a) The system of defining, amending, and installing special test equipment at RAE, Farnborough should be reviewed.

(b) Consideration should be given to improving the fire warning systems on the valiant, particularly in the "organ loft". Until such improvement is made a physical check in this area appears justified after heavy loads such as those of engine starting have been imposed.

(c) *The lessons learnt from this experience on the Valiant should be applied where necessary in a thorough review of the other "V" bombers and future aircraft.*

(d) *The methods of training crews on the Valiant at Farnborough should be further reviewed with the aim of profiting more from the facilities and methods used elsewhere.*

This report was signed by Wing Commander HJ Cundall and Flight Lieutenant VJ Glanville on 18th May 1956.

Group Captain DC McKinley the Unit Commander at Farnborough responded to the Court's findings

1. *I am confident that the accident resulted from the complete or near complete failure of the 112V. power supply and there is sufficient evidence to show the aircraft could have been consuming its 96V. reserve supply for a period prior to impact without displaying this fact to the pilot. This possibility is being examined in greater detail.*

2. *An initial scale of modifications is in train to remove the suspected root cause of this accident and an extensive examination is being made to determine if other doubtful circuits remain, the failure of which might be equally disastrous.*

3. *Whilst fully accepting the observations of the Court relating to training methods at Farnborough, I would stress the early difficulties experienced by the Ministry of Supply in preparing to fly aircraft not yet available to the Service. In this case the pilot was one initially trained in part by the aircraft manufacturers and before Gaydon became fully operative, and I am satisfied that this training was adequate. I have continued to lean heavily on Gaydon for advice, but have not so far had to call on the use of full training facilities, but I will do so when and if a further need arises.*

4. *I, too, am equally disturbed by the Captain's decision to fly low down at a relatively fast speed. However, knowing Orman as fully as I did, I have every confidence that he could have countered any reasonable difficulties associated with such flight conditions had he not been deprived of an emergency electrical supply following a very rare suspected failure.*

5. *Until every reasonable precaution has been taken to remove all sources of single point failure, the result of which might jeopardise the aircraft's safety, I believe it essential to restrict speed against altitude and I would suggest that this is no greater than 220 knots below 2,000 ft. In addition, I would question the wisdom of close formation flying at greater speeds or lower altitudes than these, bearing in mind the high stick forces imposed on the pilot should control revert to "manual". The arrangement of the trimmer controls makes it doubly difficult*

to use them during high stick forces and aileron control in manual becomes increasingly difficult as speeds rise above 180 knots.

On 26th May the Hartlepool Northern Daily Mail reported

"Valiant four-jet V-bombers flew again yesterday for the first time since the Air Ministry announced last week that pending inquiries into the crash of one on a railway embankment at Southwick, Sussex on May 11, Bomber Command Valiants would not fly. An Air Ministry spokesman said: "Modifications have to be made and as each plane is modified it will return to squadron service.""

On 30th May in the House of Commons Mr Beswick asked the Secretary for Air the reasons for the grounding of the Canberra and Valiant aircraft. Mr Birch replied that faults had been found in the electrical system which controls the tailplane actuator in the Canberra, and two Marks had been grounded while modifications were made. Flying of the Valiant was suspended as a precautionary measure after the crash in Southwick. He said certain modifications were being made to the electrical wiring system of the aircraft. Both Canberras and Valiants would be returning to flying as they were modified, and all Valiants in Bomber Command were likely to have been modified by the end of the week.

It is not disclosed what the modifications to the Valiants were. These comments in the House of Commons do highlight the fact that the electrical wiring of post war planes was still developing and that some problems only came to light in the most tragic of circumstances.

The Inquest

The official inquest into the deaths of the three crew was opened three days after the crash, on Monday 14th May, and then adjourned until the results of the Court of Inquiry were known. It reconvened on Wednesday 13th June at 4pm in Shoreham Town Hall. As well as evidence from the co-pilot, the jury heard from two technical inspectors, Mr J W Wright and Mr B A Maries that the plane was inspected three times, twice at Farnborough and once at Wisley.

"Nothing was wrong with it then".

Squadron Leader John Finch O.B.E., D.F.C., A.F.C., Wing Commander Flying at Farnborough said he examined the wreckage with experts and the general opinion of the primary cause of the crash, he said, was an electrical failure. This could not be foreseen during ordinary maintenance or in flight. The failure, he said, was in no way connected with the failure of the test equipment. He said all members of the crew were very experienced men.

Firemen examining the wreckage

The coroner, Mr Francis F. Haddock, directed the jury to return a verdict of accidental death, which they did without retiring. Mr Haddock said

"While aircraft fly, there are bound to be these crashes, and all we can hope is they will become less frequent as time goes on".

He went on to say

"No doubt the captain remained on board in order to make it as certain as possible that the occupants escaped, and to do all that he could to prevent the aircraft crashing on houses".

Of course the sad truth is that the complete failure of the electrics meant that the pilot could not control the aircraft at all and was certainly not able to aim for the recreation ground. Had he been able to steer the plane he would almost certainly have tried to steer away from a built-up area towards the sea.

The coroner also paid tribute to the public services that went to the scene of the crash, and to the ordinary citizens of Southwick.

"I went to the scene of the crash myself that Friday night and saw the people of Croft Avenue quietly and philosophically looking at their homes in a manner we remember with bomb damage during the war. I know how very gratified Wing Commander Finch, of the Royal Aircraft Establishment was with the way all the services, the police, fire and others did their work. I would like to express my tribute as well."

Part Two: The Impact on the Local Community

Destroyed homes and miraculous escapes

Although, as the Court noted,

"the injury to civilians and damage to property was miraculously small considering the circumstances"

this does not diminish from the fact that there was considerable damage to some properties and some injuries. Mr Frederick Harrison from the Air Ministry inspected the scene on Saturday 12th May and found that the following damage had been caused to civilian property: -

"Permanent way and railway fencing, extensive damage to Nos. 30 to 46 Croft Avenue, Southwick, and damage to a lesser degree to Nos. 15 to 41 and 8 to 28. Damage to the rear part of houses Nos. 27 to 59, White Rock Place, the Police House, White Rock Place, and Nos. 1 to 41, The Gardens, damage to Recreation Ground Pavilion and minor damage to a group of Council houses in Orchard Close, Manor Hall Road and Meadow Place. It is my opinion that the claim arising from this damage will amount to approximately £25,000."

Damage to the rear of houses in Croft Avenue

Some houses in Croft Avenue were declared uninhabitable and the residents were moved to other accommodation. One of the families most affected was the Guy family. Mr and Mrs Guy lived at No. 40 Croft Avenue with their three sons, Alan, Malcolm and Colin. Mrs Gladys Guy was one of the civilian casualties noted by the Court inquiry. No. 40 is on the south side of the road, very close to the entrance to the recreation ground and the garden backs on to the railway line. Mrs Guy was in her garden hanging out her washing just minutes before the crash. She had just returned indoors to her kitchen when the plane crashed showering the garden with debris and damaging the roof. The window of her sitting room shattered, and pieces of glass impaled the settee where she had been sitting not long before. Her son Colin recalls that a few seconds after the crash his mother went to check that their next-door neighbour was alright. Then she said to the neighbour that she must go back to her house as it was on fire. Colin's brother Malcolm remembers that their neighbour opposite, Mr MacPherson the dentist, later apologised to his mother for putting out a fire in their kitchen by using one of her saucepans. Mrs Guy was quoted in the Evening Argus as saying-

"I was in the garden hanging out the washing and I'd just got back into the kitchen when the explosion came. All I could see was smoke and flame. A piece of the burning plane had crashed through my kitchen window and landed on the draining board only a few feet from me. I panicked. I did not know what to do because the kitchen door had jammed and I couldn't get out. I literally thought the end of the world had come, but somehow I managed to get the door open."

She told the Shoreham Herald

"Had I hung out just one more garment on the drying line, I should have been in the middle of it all. I've still got glass in my hair from the shattered windows and I've hardly any clothes left. My house is wrecked. The French windows were blown in, together with doors and windows. I opened the airing cupboard door and saw the sky through the top. My furniture just fell to pieces."

The Worthing Herald reported that Mrs R W Guy, president of Worthing Professional and Business Women's Club, narrowly escaped death. Her home was a ruin but she was thankful it was no worse.

In 2020 her son Malcolm shared his memories of the incident with me.

"My brother Alan and I were at school in Steyning when we were informed that a plane had crashed on our house, we thought it likely to be a light aircraft from the nearby Shoreham Airport. On arrival in Croft Avenue, there were many emergency vehicles in the road but I don't recall seeing very much damage or wreckage. On entering our house, we found the rear was extremely damaged with wreckage everywhere. We learnt later that mother had been in the garden seconds before impact but fortunately had re-entered

the house. The garden was totally destroyed, all fences, the garden shed and the WW2 air-raid shelter were completely flattened. There was an unpleasant smell in the air. We had a large cherry tree in blossom which was blackened by fire, except for a small branch which had been trapped by the roof of our neighbour's garage when it was blown off by the impact."

A damaged house in Croft Avenue

His brother Alan also remembers the incident vividly

"I remember that my brother, Malcolm, and I, received permission to leave Steyning Grammar School early. We caught the only available train to the coast, but it was stopped at the level crossing by the old Adur river bridge, as there was no access to the main line by Shoreham station. We were instructed to climb down from the train and into a police car, (no handcuffs!) and were driven the remaining distance to Croft Avenue.

Once there, we were dropped off by the first house, No. 10, and walked the rest of the way to our house at No. 40. The road was full of emergency vehicles and official-looking cars and vans. The closer we got to No. 40 so the amount of wreckage on the street, in gardens, caught up in trees and telephone wires, increased. There were several broken windows, a couple of collapsed chimneys, and roofs missing tiles.

The fires had all been extinguished, but there were still many firemen, and too many photographers and journalists, around. The all-pervading memory I think we both have was the reek of burned aircraft fuel. This did not dissipate until several days later. It permeated everything in the houses closest to the point of the explosion, which was the fence between our house and No. 42.

We were able to access our house, after climbing over a small mountain of roof tiles at our front door porch. They had been blown off the back roof by the explosion. We, and all our immediate neighbours were fortunate in that all those properties were pre-WW2 built structures, with quality materials. Thus, although everything in the back gardens was incinerated, the houses themselves did not actually catch fire.

I do not recall where we spent that night, and we did not go to school the next day, which was, I think, a Saturday. We would normally have been at school for a half-day; strange system at Steyning. I do remember that we bought a copy of every national daily, and we had made the front page of them all, except the Times, which, in those days did not put news on the front page, only "In Memoriams."

Our mother, who was not injured, miraculously so, was annoyed with the reporters because in that day's papers her age was given as 47, 45, 51 and "middle" and they were all wrong!"

The youngest brother Colin was only 11 and was at Manor Hall Road School.

"I remember I was in the school playground when the plane crashed. I recall the noise the plane made and all the children who were in the playground were ushered into the school building for obvious reasons. Some time passed and other children who had had their lunch at home came back to the school. Some of them said to me that our house was a real mess.

The back part of our house was in a pretty bad state with most of the windows broken and I also recall the guttering had collapsed. The front of our home was not as bad as the back, but still it was uninhabitable. Lots of pieces of the plane were scattered around the back garden. Later that day and also other days we looked into the garden and saw the bits of plane everywhere. Needless to say we did gather a few small bits as tokens!"

The Guys were rehoused by the Council in No. 28 The Green, with Colin and Malcolm becoming temporary boarders at Steyning Grammar School.

On June 22nd the Shoreham Herald published a letter from Mr and Mrs Guy thanking the people of Southwick for their kindness and help.

"We shall be most grateful if you will allow us to thank publicly through the medium of your columns, the many organisations and individual folk who gave us so much assistance on the occasion of the Valiant Bomber crash on our home in Croft Avenue, Southwick on May 11th.

When we were instructed to evacuate our house immediately after the crash, our home was cleared and packed by many willing hands - some known and many unknown to us - in the midst of soot, glass and general debris, and the shadow of an unsafe chimney hanging over the roof. Our thanks go out to all these folks, especially the members of the Southwick Players and of the Community Association of Southwick, and also to business associates.

The official authorities and voluntary organisations have already, in these columns, received their well-earned tributes for the parts they played, and we would like to associate ourselves with all that has been said.

To the Southwick Urban Council we would like to say, "Thank you" for so quickly placing accommodation at our disposal. To our many friends in Croft Avenue and other parts of Southwick, our thanks for the help offered and for the loan of curtains, beds, etc. To Steyning Grammar School also go our thanks for so promptly accepting two of our sons as temporary boarders.

For the many, many letters of sympathy and encouragement we received during those first difficult days - our most grateful thanks and appreciation.

And finally our silent tribute to those brave men who gave their lives in their endeavour to avoid the even greater tragedy that might have been. We will always remember them. R.W. and G.E. Guy."

After the accident Mrs Guy refused to move back to Croft Avenue and they later moved to a new bungalow in Glebe Close

Next door to the Guys, at No. 38, Mrs Elsie Nicholson was preparing luncheon at her kitchen table in front of a large window when the crash occurred.

"I turned away from the window instinctively as I heard a terrific crashing noise and then every pane of glass was blown into the kitchen, showering the table. There was a big bang, but then there seemed to be others which went on and on. After that there was the noise as parts of the plane fell on the houses and all around. It was worse than anything we had in the war."

From her kitchen Mrs Nicholson could see her garage. Its roof was completely flattened by the blast and resting on top of her car.

At No. 34 Mr and Mrs G W Rampton were sitting down to lunch.

"We had the impression of a vivid orange-red burst of flame and an explosion"

They told the Shoreham Herald

Mrs Elsie Nicholson was preparing lunch in her Croft Avenue kitchen when the Valiant crashed.

"The next moment we were simply showered with splintered glass from the French doors and windows. Then there was unspeakable confusion as tiles were ripped from the roof and parts of burning aircraft fell in the garden. Some burned as they hung in the trees."

Mr Rampton paid tribute to the Women's Volunteer Service in assisting local householders to clean up debris, comforting the shocked and providing cups of tea.

Mrs K Didden of 16 Park Lane, a WVS worker was in the mouth of Croft Avenue when the plane fell.

"My impression was of huge flames in the sky and then the plane was no more. I automatically ducked as pieces fell everywhere."

John Young was a pupil at Manor Hall Road School and had gone home to his house, No. 23, on the north side of Croft Avenue for his lunch. He remembers that his mother was trying to persuade him to eat his lunch of liver when the whole house shook. In the next few days he saw miles and miles of blue cable lying on the recreation ground.

"We were told not to take it, but of course if you're told not to take it, you take it, don't you!"

The roof of a collapsed garage in Croft Avenue resting on the car (left). A fireman retrieving a piece of wreckage which had lodged in the branches of a tree.

John Young and Colin Guy weren't the only ones to collect pieces of wreckage, and in the weeks after the crash police officers visited local schools asking children to return their souvenirs. An article in the Shoreham Herald on June 1st asked people to return any parts they may have collected so that they could be examined as part of the accident investigation.

"Some bits could not be found at the scene and they are of vital importance."

At No. 22 Croft Avenue Mrs Stella Wallace and her mother were also just starting lunch.

"I heard an explosion and looked up to see what looked like a ball of flame. My mother and I rushed to the front of the house. A second later all the back windows were shattered. When we investigated the damage we found a section of the railway line in the garden."

Mrs Marjorie Inskip of 31 Croft Avenue heard the explosion but at first thought it was a bang caused by a jet plane breaking the sound barrier. The next thing that she knew was that her garden was filled with small pieces of aircraft, still burning.

Billy Atherfold, a Southwick Council official, lived with his parents on the south side of Croft Avenue in the last house before the recreation ground, No. 46. He was working in the Town Hall at the time of the crash. When he got home he found that a piece of wreckage had gone through the roof and shot through his wardrobe cutting a suit clean in half. His 82-year-old mother was alone in the house when the plane crashed. She was badly shocked and shaken by the blast and was one of the official listed civilian casualties, along with Mrs Guy, Mrs Guest, an unknown male and Mrs Parker.

Wreckage still smouldering in Croft Avenue. Photo by Peter Sayer

Another piece of wreckage, a heavy aluminium casting, tore through Mrs Rhoda Guest's house, No. 42, piercing two walls at the south-east corner and slicing through the chimney inside. It then hit No. 44 and landed in the kitchen. No. 44 belonged to Billy Atherfold's sister and brother-in-law Mr and Mrs D Smith.

Mr E A Coates, Southwick Council Surveyor, lived in the last house on the north side of Croft Avenue at No. 41. He had to climb up to his roof to put out a small fire. He said

"Burning wreckage landed on the roof, melting lead flashing."

Otherwise his house was undamaged and he opened it as a temporary headquarters for the RAF personnel and other departments.

Mr Coates also complimented the police on their thoroughness when dealing with the aftermath of the crash. They sealed off Croft Avenue from sightseers and set up an incident post. A special police van was brought to the scene and a flagpole and blue flag hoisted. The van was equipped with radio which enabled them to keep in touch with their headquarters. They helped with the recovery of the bodies and maintained an all-night guard on the wreckage. They also dealt with the additional burden of a flood of telephone calls, which came from all over the country from people anxious about relatives. They wanted the police to check if their relatives were safe and then ring back.

Shoreham and Southwick Civil Defence personnel were also quickly on the scene. Two years previously they had actually taken part in an exercise designed to show members what action to take in the event of an aircraft crashing in Southwick. When the real thing happened they swung smoothly into action. The rescue section went through the wrecked buildings and members of the wardens' and headquarters' sections reported for duty. At the beginning of the month lectures had been held on how to deal with ejector seats in crashed aircraft. Mr H A Hoar, of Underdown Road, together with Mr S A Towner, of Brighton, was going through the damaged properties to see that everyone was safe when he discovered an ejector seat complete with its explosive charge. He was a former flight lieutenant in the RAF and was engaged in dealing with crashes when in service. He erected a barricade around the ejector seat and chalked a "danger" notice on it. He also collected and identified parts of wreckage which might be needed for the investigation. Mr Hoar was commended by the RAF for his actions in isolating the undischarged ejector seat. The seat must have belonged to the pilot Captain Orman, as the other two crew did not have ejector seats.

The local medical officer Dr Tom Harrison happened to be receiving treatment from the dentist Mr MacPherson in No. 35 Croft Avenue, on the north side of the road, when the crash occurred. He quickly set up a first aid post with the help of the dentist. Mrs MacPherson provided cups of tea for her neighbours. She, like many others, thought it was a bomb.

"There was a flash and a woof and pieces showered down all over the place"

The injuries were mainly scratches and shock. The only civilian who had to go to Southlands Hospital to be treated was Mrs Margaret Parker of Brighton Road, Shoreham, who had been walking her dog in the recreation ground. She was treated for minor burns, then allowed to go home. The local St John Ambulance Brigade were also quickly on the scene, as were the Women's Volunteer Service. They set up an information office in the garden of one of the damaged houses and prepared and served tea and sandwiches to police and RAF personnel on duty at the crash site. The "feeding party" prepared the food and drinks at the Civil Defence headquarters in Kingston Lane. To provide sufficient boiling water quickly they built outdoor fires according to emergency procedures. They also went round to the shattered homes to make sure there were no injured left unattended in them.

Mrs I MacPherson holding wreckage which flew past her as she was coming in from the garden.

Whilst Croft Avenue bore the brunt of the damage, houses in Whiterock Place, on the south side of the railway line, also suffered damage from the blast and hurtling debris. Luckily no one was in their gardens and the only injuries were bruises and shock. The Shoreham Herald reported

"One woman who escaped death by inches was Mrs Ruby Sturmey of No. 39. She was cleaning in a small outhouse outside the kitchen and had just stepped inside to attend to the gas stove when the plane exploded. A great piece of debris crashed through the outhouse roof right by her. The only injury she received was a severe graze on one arm as she was blown through the doorway of the kitchen by the blast.

Her husband, Mr Arthur Sturmey, former Southwick and Sussex goalkeeper, usually returns home from work at the Sussex Yacht Club, Shoreham, at about 12.30 pm and spends half an hour on his allotment by the side of the railway bank before going in for dinner. On Friday he stayed on at work longer to finish a job and was not home when the crash came. "If I had followed my usual routine" he told the Herald, "I should have been on my allotment where the plane crashed. The garden was coming along beautifully," he said surveying the mass of wreckage which smothered the growing plants, "and I had spent Thursday evening putting in pea sticks." As sightseers crowded in the entry between Mr Sturmey's home and the former police station, which had windows blown in and the roof damaged, neighbours swept up the broken glass and cleared away the mess in their homes. Assessors were busy at work making notes of the damage."

The south side of the railway embankment looking east towards the footbridge over the railway

Eyewitness accounts

Ernie Goodman was working on an expansion joint on the roof of the power station when he saw the plane coming in very low over the sea from the west. In 2003 he dictated his memories to the Southwick Society.

"It was not on fire as some people have said since, but there were coloured Very lights coming from it, maybe they were some sort of distress signal. I could see the plane very clearly because it was so close.

It was flying towards the locks. At that time they were building the Prince Philip Lock and there were several tall cranes there. It seemed that it must hit the cranes. At the last moment the plane banked to one side and missed them. There was a train in Southwick Station; it was fortunate that it had not started for Brighton a few moments earlier.

The plane hit the railway line and bounced. There was a huge explosion, a flash, fire and smoke. Pieces of wreckage were flying everywhere. I was frantic because we were living at 1 White Rock Place. My wife had just had our daughter and was at home with her. I ran from the power station and took the ferryboat across the Canal and ran home. When I got home my wife was shaking and frightened. Our daughter was still asleep in the pram outside! Both were unhurt. There was a lot of damage to houses; it was just like the war.

Southwick has had a lot of near misses. There was the bomb that dropped by the church and didn't go off. There were several other bombs during the war that did not go off."

At Manor Hall Road School Mike Shoulders was in the playground and saw the plane crash. He remembers

"There were about twelve of us in the playground at Manor Hall Road School. All the others were inside having lunch or had gone home, I had brought sandwiches, which is how I came to be outside. I had a brief and blurred impression of a plane coming in very low and fast; it could have been a flying saucer! There was a huge bang as it hit the ground. A large round piece of wreckage landed in the playground. It was round and several feet across; it could have been part of the engine fan or cowling. When it was all over the playground was covered in nuts and bolts and many small pieces of metal. The explosion must have been enormous to send debris from Croft Avenue to the school.

A teacher came and found us and told us off for being in the playground. They had sent everybody else out into the street on the other side of the school, but we hadn't known that. We didn't get sent home in the afternoon but we were not allowed out in the playground at 3.00 o'clock, which was playtime."

Another pupil, Mike Peacock, remembers he felt a big thumping crash on the ground one lunch hour. He lived in The Crescent to the north of the recreation ground, but it was such a thump that the top bolt of their French windows unbolted itself.

"Word soon got around that a warplane had crashed and the crew were killed. We were not allowed to talk about it at school. The recreation ground was out of bounds. The following week-end, I was on the train from Southwick to Brighton which passes the southern boundary of the recreation ground. All of the grass surface was completely littered with wreckage. The whole mess was cleaned up amazingly quickly and the park was back in use in no time. The other fear at the time was that the bomber was carrying nuclear bombs!"

Terry Langrish, also a pupil at Manor Hall Road School, didn't like school dinners so was having his lunchtime chips with his mother in their house in Orchard Close. He says that the explosion was the loudest noise he had ever heard and rattled the door and windows so violently that he was sure they would come crashing in. His mum, Lily, screamed

"Oh my God, the power station's blown up!"

She could see from her house across the recreation ground huge clouds of black smoke coming from the direction of the power station, where her husband was at work.

Terry's mum was not the only Southwick resident to think this. My mother-in law Linda Candy, who lived in Manor Hall Road, had the same thought and like many wives feared for her husband working there. As it happened her husband Ken was already on his way home for his lunch. He said that as he cycled up Southwick Street he heard the noise of a jet plane, and then a bang which must have been the co-pilot ejecting from the stricken plane. He looked up but couldn't see anything as the plane was already too low to see over the houses.

A compressor disc which sliced into the ground and an undercarriage wheel

Terry and his mum ran down their garden towards the hole in their hedge which led into the recreation ground. Terry remembers

"I was halted in my tracks by noises seemingly coming from the ground around me and a strange metallic 'tinkling' sound coming from the roof tiles of all the neighbouring houses and as I looked up I saw a large disc spinning through the air alongside a long metal tube which struck neighbouring houses. As I followed mum (through the hedge) I was greeted with a scene of utter devastation across the whole rec. Huge landing wheels were bouncing along the grass and smashing into the timber of the Southwick Football Club's grandstand; a large coil of wires was rolling along burning furiously; an electrical conductor rail from the railway line was bizarrely standing vertically with huge blue sparks shooting up and down its length. There were many small and large fires burning everywhere and as we ran on into the middle of the rec we were surrounded by large amounts of wreckage, mostly small but some large pieces of twisted and shattered aircraft sections. Mum was terrified that children returning to school from lunch would be caught in this disaster and she ran into the middle of the debris field searching desperately for anyone who may have been injured or worse. By this time people were streaming into the rec from all sides and at that point mum bumped into Mr Harding, the taxi driver from over the bridge, and I overheard an exchange between them saying they had both seen torsos of what they assumed to be aircrew. Emergency vehicles then started to arrive in droves and, excitement over, we headed back home through the hedge".

Onlookers examining larger pieces of wreckage on Southwick Recreation Ground.
Photo by Peter Sayer

That evening Terry and his brothers looked out of their bedroom window

"We could see men in gabardine macs, carrying what looked like machine-guns, patrolling close to our house all night long. Apparently there was some top-secret

equipment aboard the aircraft and at school the headmaster called the whole school together and said that if any boys had picked up mementoes of the wrecked aircraft they should be brought to school and placed outside his office immediately."

This produced a bit of a competition amongst the children to see who could bring in the largest pieces possible, not all of them necessarily from the air crash! Even so some pieces never made their way to the investigators but were kept as souvenirs.

Press attention

The crash, of course, caught the attention of the press, both local and national. The Valiant was described in several newspapers as the Million Pound Plane. The Evening Argus stated

"The Valiant is the £1 million nuclear weapon plane which can provide as much punch as could the whole of Bomber Command during the war. It was on show for the first time in March. Three RAF squadrons are so far equipped with it. The cream of the RAF aircrew are being trained to fly the four-jet machine."

The Shoreham Herald described the scene in Croft Avenue.

"Over a large part of its length Croft Avenue was scattered with small pieces of wreckage, wireless equipment and gearwheels. Pieces which were on fire had burnt small holes in the road surface. In the gardens more wreckage was scattered, a tree in one holding a sheet of metal about five by three feet in its branches. Both in the gardens and on the roadway itself were fragments of stone ballast which had been blasted from the railway line. Burning wreckage set light to garages, garden sheds and outhouses on the backs of houses. Householders, after the initial shock of the crash, brought out watering cans and buckets filled with water to douse the flames."

A reporter who saw the explosion told the Evening Argus

"There was the noise of an aircraft travelling across Shoreham. There followed two minor explosions and then a terrific bang. A ball of flame, crimson coloured and mingled with smoke, mushroomed 50ft into the air. There was an indescribable scene in Croft Avenue, a quiet backwater leading to the recreation ground. The avenue was ankle deep in broken glass and rubble."

The Evening Argus also described a search at sea.

"Two helicopters and a Wyvern aircraft took part in the search off the coast for a member of crew who was believed to have bailed out. The Vigo, a gunnery training ship, the Starling, a navigational training ship, the frigate Loch Killisport, the minelayer Plover and the coastal minesweepers Brigham, Bodenham, Chelsham, Ledsham and Altham and Shoreham lifeboat all took part".

Part of the fuselage in the trees on the railway embankment.

Several newspapers reported that the Shoreham lifeboat picked up the body of a member of the crew who landed in the sea. However, this could not have been the case, as only the co-pilot bailed out and he landed in some allotments. The other crew members were all still in the plane when it crashed. Their bodies were identified by Squadron Leader William Colebeck, Station Medical Officer, Farnborough.

"All three bodies had suffered very serious multiple injuries and death must have been instantaneous."

The Shoreham Herald of 18th May reported that a body of one of the airmen was found at No. 40 Croft Avenue, still with his unopened parachute on him. This may well have been where Mr Hoar found the undischarged ejector seat. I asked Alan Guy, whose family lived at No. 40, if he knew if this was true. He said

"As for the corpse, that may well be true. The point of the explosion was at the fence between us and No. 42, the other half of our semi-detached. Neither of us saw a body being transported out of what was left of the back garden, but when we first got there the

space was full of uniforms and wreckage and still, smoke, and the roadway was almost wall to wall emergency vehicles".

He also said that there was a rumour that

"some months after the crash, when the workmen who had done the renovation on No. 40 were spreading out the ashes from a large bonfire which they had built down on what used to be the vegetable garden, one of them dug up a whole human arm".

Squadron Leader Colebeck also examined Flight Lieutenant Preece following the accident.

"He suffered five superficial lacerations of the scalp, a sprain of his left knee and bruising of his left arm and thigh. These injuries are consistent with a heavy parachute landing on a hard surface."

*A policeman examining the flying helmet of one of the crew killed in the crash.
Photo by Peter Sayer*

The allotments where he landed were north of Butts Road, near Jack Creswell's grocer's shop and the old station ticket office. Mrs Eileen d'Eathe of

Millcroft Road saw the parachute leave the plane and thought

"Thank God, one of them got out alive."

Bus conductor Albert Stoughton, of Steyning Avenue, Hove, also saw the co-pilot bale out just before the plane crashed. His bus, a No. 4, was standing at The Green in Southwick, waiting to start its journey to Rottingdean. He told the Brighton & Hove Herald reporter

"I felt the terrific heat of the burning plane as it passed a few feet over us. I thought it was going to scorch the bus. Then I saw one of the crew bale out. He turned over and over, then his parachute opened. But he was so near the ground that I thought he must have been killed. The children playing in the school opposite screamed as the plane went over. It flew very close to the school roof."

The newspaper reported that the aircraft missed Southwick Junior Girls School (The Green School) by only a few feet. There may be some dramatic licence in this description of events, as the plane wasn't on fire before it crashed and from other evidence it seems doubtful that the plane actually came far enough inland to fly over the school roof.

The Evening Argus reported

"Blonde Miss Moyra Sherwood, aged 25, of Butts Road, Southwick, was one of the first to go to the aid of the pilot, who landed by parachute in an allotment at the rear of her house. She was in the kitchen with her mother and saw the drama through the back window. "I dashed straight out when I saw him coming down" she said. "As I raced down the road I saw his handkerchief flutter down and get caught up on a fence. I picked it up. Then I noticed his wristwatch by the side of the road and I took that to him as well. He did not seem very badly hurt – a bit dazed – but blood was trickling from a cut on his head. I went up to him and said have you lost a watch? Looking back on it it must have been a silly thing to say to a man who had just missed losing his life by the skin of his teeth."

The Belfast News reported that the co-pilot was still in his ejector seat when he was found. Miss Annie Sharp, of Butts Road, told the Evening Argus that she saw the ejector seat strike the roof of Southwick Railway Station, so it is possible he hit the ticket office roof before falling into the next-door allotments. Miss Sharp said

"The man on the parachute crashed through a wire fence round the nearby allotments. He was groaning and calling for water. He appeared to have a bad cut on the back of his head."

The co-pilot's ejector seat and parachute

St John Ambulance man Mr George Shuttleworth, of Cross Road, used his knife to cut the pilot free from the ejector seat with the assistance of Jack Creswell the greengrocer. The pilot asked them

"What has happened to the others? Are they alright?"

The pilot was initially taken to the nearby station for first aid then he was taken to Southlands Hospital, Shoreham. Mr Shuttleworth reported that when they were at the station

"He telephoned Farnborough, but it was a top-secret message and he spoke in code."

The Valiant was, of course, a very new military weapon and there were also reports, in the Brighton & Hove Herald, of top-secret documents, films and maps being rescued from the crash scene and bundled hurriedly into the back of a police car.

There were many stories of the miraculous escapes the people of Southwick had had. The Evening Argus reported how close the plane had come to crashing on to a train.

"Motorman Arthur Collins, of Picton Street, Brighton was driving an electric train from West Worthing when he saw the plane plunge on the track ahead of him. He clapped on his brakes immediately. 'I saw a brilliant white flash and then a mushroom of smoke billow up', he told a reporter. Commentated his guard, Mr Thomas Guile, of Franklin Street, Brighton: 'If we had been even a minute ahead of schedule we would have been right under it.'"

Another eyewitness, Mr Sidney Sopp, of Southwick, was standing on the railway bridge east of the crash scene. He said

"I saw an orange ball of fire racing towards me. Then came the explosion. Wreckage was strung in trees and littered gardens with white-hot metal."

Mr Sopp was lucky not to be injured as David Cross, who was a schoolboy at Manor Hall Junior School, remembers that a piece of wreckage had gone right through the middle of the bridge. It was closed after the accident but he sneaked a look when no one was around and saw quite a large hole. David Cross also recalls that he was at his Nan's house in Manor Hall Road having lunch when the crash occurred.

Policemen examining the train track. The footbridge Mr Sopp was standing on can be seen in the background.

"There was a colossal bang and the ground shook. My Nan went under the dining table; later she told me it reminded her of bombs dropping in the war."

David walked back to school with his friend Allan Uwins. As they entered the recreation ground by the tennis courts they saw bits of aircraft everywhere, all sorts of shapes and sizes. There was no one to stop them and they walked parallel to the tennis courts along the path and could see wreckage on and near the railway line. The fencing of the tennis courts had big hollows in it in various places where bits of the aircraft had been caught in it, which was very lucky for the houses that were just beyond the tennis courts.

Heather Herridge, who was only 4 in 1956, attended Fishersgate Infants School. She recalls that she would normally make her way home from school across the footbridge from Eastbrook Way to the recreation ground to meet her mother who was waiting.

"She had just had my younger sister and wheeled her in an enormous coach-built pram, so I had to cross the bridge on my own and meet her in the Rec. With luck, I would normally be allowed to play in the rec on the way home."

Although Heather does not remember hearing the crash she says that when they came to go home all the children had to go to the old iron bridge at Fishersgate station to cross the line and meet her mum.

A scene of devastation on Southwick Recreation ground. One of the photographs sent to the Daily Mirror by Peter Sayer

"I can't remember how we were organised to go to Fishersgate bridge, whether we were guided by teachers or other mums or whether I just followed the crowd. Some arrangements must have been made otherwise my mum would not have known where I would be."

A semi-professional photographer, Peter Sayer, was working on a photo shoot at the site of the lighthouse on Kingston Beach when he saw the plane rapidly lose height and crash somewhere to his east, over central Southwick. He immediately rushed up the beach and flagged down a passing bus. He told the driver he didn't know exactly where he wanted to go but just wanted to head in the direction of the downed aircraft. At Station Road he saw an ambulance turning north towards the station. He left the bus and hurried up the road in time to see the co-pilot, with his parachute, being helped into the ambulance outside the old station forecourt. Unfortunately he didn't think to take a photograph of the co-pilot but hurried under the railway bridge and right into Croft Avenue. He took photographs of the smouldering wreckage littering the street in Croft Avenue, the damage to the houses and of larger items of wreckage in the recreation ground. He also took a picture of part of the fuselage hanging in a tree on the railway embankment and of a policeman examining the flying helmet and charts of one of the crew who were killed in the crash.

As he was the first photographer on the scene he telephoned the Daily Mirror news and picture desk and told them he had these pictures, and did they want an exclusive? They said yes and suggested he should get the pictures on the next train to London, where a courier would meet the train at Victoria Station. Peter took a taxi to Brighton Station but he had just missed the London train. He called the Daily Mirror again and they told him to bring them up by road directly to the newspaper offices. They said they would pay the fare. Peter did not arrive in time for the pictures to appear in the Southern edition of the paper, but they were used in the Northern edition.

The aftermath

Southwick Urban District Council were praised in the Shoreham Herald for their swift action on house repairs. The Council quickly issued a statement

"If your house has suffered any damage, you should first inspect your insurance policy and ascertain whether your property is covered for damage by aircraft. If it is, you should notify your insurance company that damage has been occasioned at the property. If you are not covered, notification should be addressed to the Air Ministry Directorate of Works. No repairs other than those sufficient to make the property wind and watertight, that is repairs to glazing and replacement of tiles, should be carried out. The repair of all other damage must await inspection by either the insurance company, or the Air Ministry in the case of uninsured properties."

Examining the damage to a Croft Avenue house

Almost immediately the Council started organising first aid repairs in the damaged houses. Mr A R Shott, Clerk to the Council, received co-operation from the local builders.

"Within a quarter of an hour after the "all clear" was given four building firms' representatives were in Croft Avenue taking instructions and within an hour all four firms were at work. The firms concerned are Gates of Shoreham; V L Miles Ltd of Southwick; J J Harland and Partners of Southwick; and George Comber Ltd of Portslade."

Mr Shott said the Council arranged to borrow houses to accommodate families whose homes were made unsafe, but only one family, the Guys, was affected. Mrs Rhoda Guest, of No. 42, arranged to stay with friends. All council staff available were pressed into service to make a survey of the damage for the Air Ministry's information. One of the main problems facing the Council was how to clear the recreation ground of the thousands of small pieces of metal scattered over it by the crash.

"A lot of the metal used in aircraft today is non-ferrous, and therefore cannot be picked up by magnets. How we are going to deal with the problem we don't yet know. But we are anticipating a gay old time getting mowers repaired after every cutting"

The task of clearing all the debris fell to the RAF Unit 71 who completed the clearance in a week.

All the debris was cleared from the recreation ground by Unit 71 of the RAF

The railway line was, amazingly, cleared and repaired even more quickly, with trains running again within 24 hours of the crash. The Littlehampton Gazette reported

"Trains from Littlehampton and Portsmouth to Brighton were cancelled because the Valiant had ripped up more than 200 yards of track. Copies of evening papers coming from Brighton were late in arriving in town. Some read of the crash in the stop press of a London evening paper and gathered in a group at the barrier of Littlehampton station anxiously waiting for friends and relatives to arrive from work further down the line. As soon as news of the accident came through to Littlehampton station a notice board was put up which stated that owing to circumstances beyond the control of the railway authorities the line to Shoreham was not in use. For a time traffic was brought virtually to a standstill, but later a shuttle service to stations on either side of the crash was set up. In the evening a British Railways' spokesman stated that the line would not be clear for at least 24 hours, but emergency crews working through Friday night cleared away debris and twisted metal and re-laid track so that the first train could pass through the area at 5 am on Saturday morning – 17 hours later."

The torn and twisted rails where the bomber struck

Accident investigators and emergency services examining the wreckage on the railway track

At 5.25 am the first train passed through Southwick. Trains had to move slowly along the fresh track and passengers were able to see for themselves the devastation that the crash had caused. They must also have been able to see the crash investigators who were still surveying the wreckage along the line.

Protests against low flying jets

Amazingly only four days before the Valiant crashed on Southwick Recreation Ground, a Canberra jet bomber WT 328 had crashed in the sea off Shoreham. The tail plane actuator failed, the port wing hit the water and the aircraft cartwheeled into the sea three miles south of Shoreham during low altitude altimeter trials. The wreckage was recovered by salvage vessels and towed to Portsmouth dockyard on Tuesday May 15th, to be handed over to the Ministry of Supply for examination. The missing crew were not found. The fact that both these planes were on test flights was not known by the public.

Two jet bombers crashing in one week caused great consternation in the local community. When Southwick Urban District Council met on Tuesday May 22nd for their annual meeting Councillor T J Marsh tabled a "notice of motion", calling for a protest to be made to the Air Minister concerned about the low flying planes over the town and excessive noise, such as the breaking of the sound barrier. Councillor Marsh had given an interview to the Shoreham Herald after the Valiant crash in which he explained that this action was not been taken as a direct result of the crash, although it lent weight to his proposals. He said

"during the canvassing of the area for the recent local government elections a lot of people complained about low-flying and the noise from the breaking of the sound barrier.... The crash on Friday and the one in the sea earlier the same week, seems to lead to the fact that this area is being used for the testing of experimental aircraft."

Councillor Marsh added that he was not against progress or development and that the firm for which he worked was often engaged in making parts for new planes.

His motion also called for a ban on experimental aircraft flying over or near built-up areas; for the Minister to review the arrangements for carrying out repairs to properties damaged by aircraft and to ensure that immediate authority was available for local authorities, or others, to make good the damage without delay; and that the M.P. for Arundel and Shoreham (Captain Henry Kerby) be asked to request a statement from the Minister in the House on these points. Mr Marsh said that he had not organised a petition but would do so if necessary. He said the Rector of Kingston Buci, the Rev. T Glaisyer had offered to do what he could to get his parishioners to sign a petition if one was started. The Rector had written to Councillor Marsh stating

"If all the people in Greater London (8-10,000,000) stopped at one moment and shouted at the tops of their voices, the noise would be no louder than the noise of a jet hurtling through the air at the speed of sound."

Councillor Marsh said noise of this nature affected the old, the sick, the blind, young children and expectant mothers.

"If tests and flying of this character are needed, there should be plenty of space on the Atlantic coast in areas less inhabited."

Councillor J A White supported Councillor Marsh and pointed out that there were ranges for testing atom bombs and rockets, why not ranges for experimental aircraft? However, Councillor G Hollis-Dennis said the first part of the motion was

"unsound reason in this modern day. Low flying is not a habit indulged in by a lot of young fools – they went out with string bags (older types of aircraft). Modern pilots are highly trained young men who are chosen psychologically. They take a million pounds worth of plane into the air and do not take liberties with them or their own lives. Aircraft have got to be flown low over areas where they can be expected to be used tactically. It was because the pilots in the Battle of Britain knew their terrain that they were so successful. There has ceased to be a built-up area so far as planes are concerned. In the time it takes Councillor Penney to light his pipe, an aircraft flying at 600mph can be miles away."

Despite his objection to the motion he added

"I hate aircraft and loathe them with all my feelings. I would not go up in one for all the tea in China. They are the most miserable invention of mankind. Just as the medieval people feared the plague, we fear planes."

Suspicion and fear of new technology seemed prevalent amongst the councillors. Mr V L Miles said he had been told by a responsible official that within some 15 years pilotless guided missiles will be shooting over to America with passengers aboard made unconscious by hypodermic needle injections, timed so that they would "come to" as soon as they arrived.

Councillor Hollis-Dennis then moved an amendment cutting out the first part of the motion dealing with protests against low flying and experimental planes.

Councillor Penney said he understood low flying aircraft did not break the sound barrier, which was done at heights of 40,000ft or more. He claimed too that neither of the two planes which crashed recently were experimental types. He supported the amendment and suggested the motion be put before the finance committee so that specific cases could be quoted in the request for machinery to deal with the damage. The amendment was passed nine votes to two. At the end of debate it was placed on record the Council's appreciation of the work done by the men of the 71 Unit, RAF, in clearing the debris from the recreation ground. They also expressed sympathy with the relatives of the three men who died in the Valiant and their appreciation of all who helped in the crash.

One of Councillor Marsh's demands when he put forward his notice of motion was that the Minister should review the arrangements for carrying out repairs to properties damaged by aircraft and to give authority to local authorities, or others, to make good the damage without delay. That was only 11 days after the crash. Two months later on 13th July the Shoreham Herald reported that two of the houses badly damaged in the resulting blast were nowhere near habitable, and in others the occupants were living in one or two rooms, surrounded by debris, charred furniture and pitted linen.

"Among these people there is a feeling of frustration, discontent and, as one person put it, "nasty temper" – all because they do not yet know where they stand financially."

Homeowners were still awaiting final assessments of the damage to their property.

"Apart from the uncertainty and discomfort in which these people are living, there are a number of questions uppermost in their minds; who is going to pay the professional fees involved for private assessors, architects and others?; What about the capital value of the houses?; How can we avoid being out of pocket over all this?."

The Herald had heard that for some of the people whose houses had been assessed compensation was likely to be only on the value of the article at the time it was damaged or destroyed. Also the cost of repairs would not include things such as repainting.

Mrs Rhoda Guest owned 42 Croft Avenue, one of the pair most badly hit. Her son said he expected settlement soon for the repairs to the building and furniture damaged but pointed out that it will cost more to replace the damaged articles than the amount at which they were assessed.

"I believe insurers feel they will not get enough money from the Air Ministry and are covering themselves. So far as I'm aware, no Air Ministry assessor has been near the property, or if he did, he did not inform us. The house will not be habitable until about October, and my mother, in the meantime is running around living at different addresses. We are trying to be honest about our claim, because we have a conscience, but we shall be out of pocket by the time it is settled, apart from the fact that the house will never be the same."

Mr P P Cottier, whose wife owned No. 44, told the Herald no contract had yet been awarded to a builder to repair the house.

"The value of this house will be very considerably depreciated through the repairs when they are done, and if ever it is put up for sale the price will drop. But I can't say the Air Ministry has been anything but helpful."

Mr V L Miles, a Southwick councillor, and one of the builders engaged on the repair work, said that he had carried out £3,000 worth of repairs but had only received £93 for one small job, for which the Air Ministry paid him directly. He thought that the problem lay in the number of people each claim had to pass through. Southwick Council had been urging the Ministers responsible to set up a separate body to deal with the claims on the same basis as was done in the war. One resident said

"They seem to forget we are human and all we have been through. I feel like screaming every time I hear a jet go overhead and have been ordered away by my doctor. But I can't leave until all this is settled."

By the beginning of September the Herald was reporting that nearly all the external repairs to the damaged houses had been completed but it would be another six to seven weeks before the interiors were back to normal. Some homeowners were, however, still dissatisfied that the compensation for contents was on their depreciated value.

"Many people find themselves with curtains, chair covers, bed linen and towels all pitted with tiny burns. Although an item of this nature may have only one hole in it, no self-respecting housewife would use it on her table, chair or bed."

Part Three: The Wider Picture
British Soviet relations

Whilst the development of the V-Bombers was a direct result of the fear of the Soviet Union, diplomatic efforts were being made to improve relations between the two countries. In April 1956, the month before the Valiant crash, the Soviet leaders Nicholas Bulganin and Nikita Khrushchev visited Britain to hold talks with Prime Minister Anthony Eden. As part of this visit the Soviet Minister for Power Stations, the former Prime Minister Georgi Malenkov, visited Southwick Power Station as part of a tour of Britain's power stations. Mr Malenkov stayed at the Grand Hotel in Brighton for the weekend and in the evening held an informal supper party in his suite, to which Councillor J F Fowler J.P. Chairman of Southwick Council and Mr A R Shott, the Clerk, were invited. Mr Fowler told the Shoreham Herald

"We were cordially greeted by the Russians and had an interesting evening's discussion."

I found it ironic that on the one hand Britain was developing nuclear bombers to use against the Soviets, on the other hand they were showing them the secrets of our power stations.

Georgi Malenkov, Soviet Minister for Power Stations (middle right), talking to Southwick B Power Station workers.

Dangerous times in the skies

Even before that Friday lunchtime, when a plane plummeted out of the sky onto the railway line, there had been a fear amongst the general public about the advances in modern aviation. The new jet planes were far noisier than anything that went before them. By the 1950s, many combat aircraft could routinely break the sound barrier in level flight. Protests about the sonic booms caused by aircraft breaking the sound barrier were common. Mr A Hirst of 42 Lancing Park, Lancing wrote to the Worthing Gazette in July 1956.

"Sir – I have made repeated complaints to the present Minister for Air and his predecessor direct and through our very able local M.P. regarding unbearable aeroplane noises over Lancing but no notice has been taken. In fact, since my complaints the recent crash at Southwick has happened. The machine (a Valiant) crossed my address less than 500ft up then already in trouble. In fact it appears that since our complaints we are being victimised. It is quite a usual occurrence for jet planes to circle a dozen times less than 1000ft up over our particular road obviously having been acquainted with the complainants' address.

Surely these manoeuvres could easily be carried out over the sea being less than 50 yards away and ensure survival to the pilot and crew and inhabitants. It is quite impossible to carry on a conversation on the phone or without the phone for that matter.

We are determined to have peaceful occupation of our homes and if our complaints are ignored legal action will be taken. Even during the war we were not subjected to such infernal nuisance"

And as we have seen several members of Southwick Council were also very concerned about the noise of the jet planes. As was the rector of St Julian's Church.

The fact that the Southwick Civil defence had actually carried out exercises preparing for an aircraft crash also says a lot about the worry over modern aeroplanes. All these fears weren't unfounded. Amazingly, the Valiant was the 139th UK Military aircraft loss in 1956, a total which would rise to 378 by the end of the year. Although many of these losses were caused by accidents on the runway during take-off or landing, this is still a staggering average of more than one military plane lost every day. It says a lot about the bravery of the RAF crew who flew in these aircraft.

In the first five months of 1956, before the Southwick crash, fifty crew and civilians had been killed in military crashes. Just in Sussex there were at least seven accidents. Four planes were written off in accidents at Ford aerodrome. On 20th January the pilot of a Meteor NF12 carried out an unauthorised flight over his parent's village of Wadhurst, Sussex. While in a turn at 25ft the aircraft struck a bungalow, crashed and burst into flames. Both crew and two people in the bungalow were killed. On 24th April a Sea Hawk F2 performed a slow roll at 20,000 ft and while inverted the pilot's seat was felt to move. There was a loud bang and the pilot found himself in free air still in his seat. He parachuted to safety but was injured. The aircraft crashed at Summers Place north of Billingshurst, Sussex. And then of course there was the Canberra B(I)8 which crashed into the sea three miles south of Shoreham on 7th May killing both its crew.

The Meteor flight over his parent's village was not the only unauthorised flight which resulted in the loss of a plane. A Hunter F2 was lost in March when a pilot took off from Wattisham for a night cross-country sortie, apparently intending to carry out an unauthorised flight over a lighthouse in the Thames Estuary, but never returned. These unauthorised flights explain why one of the terms of reference of the Court of Inquiry was establishing that all members of the crew were on duty at the time of the accident.

Ejector seats for the rear crew

The Investigating Officer Mr Nowak's report to the Court of Inquiry stated that

"Due to lack of evidence on the harness and the fact that, so far, I have not been able to establish whether or not the crew escape door had been jettisoned, I am unable to say how far the occupants had progressed with their escape drill."

Evans and Knight had no ejector seats but had parachutes, and there was a door in the left-hand side of the plane through which they had to jump out. When the Valiant was designed it was felt that it was not technically feasible to provide ejector seats for the three rear crew members. One of the reasons was that the rear crew sit with their backs to the pilots and there was a technical problem of spinning them round on ejection. Also the bombers were designed to fly at high altitudes which would, of course, give the crew greater time and height to escape by parachute. By the 1960s the bombers were required to fly at lower levels. As the crash at Southwick proved, ejector seats can save lives from very low levels, where a parachute would probably prove useless.

In June 1964 the provision of ejector seats for the rear crew was discussed in the House of Lords. The Earl of Kinnoull asked Her Majesty's Government whether, in view of the increasing number of Royal Aire Force personnel killed in V-Bomber accidents, they would reconsider the decision to supply only the pilot and co-pilot with ejector seats. He referred to the crash on 11th May 1 964 of a Vulcan bomber, on the approach to landing, where the three rear crew members were killed whilst the two pilots, having ejected at a very low level, survived.

Starboard escape hatch and emergency exit door.

"This accident triggered off yet again a feeling among many people concerned with these aircraft as to the question: is it morally right to continue to send up air crews in V-Bombers, knowing full well that if the aircraft gets into difficulties at low level the crew have next to no chance of baling out? Does not the benefit of hindsight prove to-day how utterly wrong was the decision taken four years ago not to adapt the V-Bombers with ejector seats?"

In his reply Lord Shackleton referred to the crash at Southwick.

"As the noble Earl said, the present situation is really an almost impossible one. We have already example after example of a pilot being saved and the rear crew losing their lives or, alternatively, of the pilot going voluntarily to his death along with the rear crew. There is one case of which I am aware, and of which no doubt the noble Lord who is to reply is equally aware, of a Valiant which had a complete electrical failure at 1,000 feet and it was quite impossible to get the aircraft under control. The second pilot ejected and the pilot remained with his aircraft and went to his death".

Despite these discussions in the House of Lords and a succession of design suggestions, from ejector seat manufactures Martin Baker Ltd, rear ejector seats were never fitted to the V-bombers. The decision not to fit them was a mixture of prohibitive cost and the fear of taking any of our nuclear deterrent out of action for up to eight months for the seats to be fitted.

Fred Jones' crash investigation book

The Court of Inquiry, concerned with the need to speedily make recommendations as to the safety of other Valiant bombers, concluded after only 7 days and before investigations into the electrical failures had been completed. Despite Wing Commander Finch's declaration at the inquest in June that the failure was in no way connected with the failure of the test equipment, there have been later suggestions that maybe if not the equipment then, at least, the operator of the equipment may have been the cause of the accident.

Fred Jones was one of the air accident investigators involved with the crash investigation. In 1985 he published a book, *"Air Crash" The Clues in the Wreckage,* in which he claimed that the constant resetting of the circuit breaker by Mr Knight disrupted the electrical supplies in the bomber, and therefore, led to the crash. Mr Jones wrote

"this particular type of aeroplane was rather unique: its controls were fully electrically operated and not by some form of hydraulic power assistance as with other contemporary aeroplanes of such a large size.

As a type, this bomber has been flying quite successfully and had never experienced loss of control due to major electrical failure. As far as possible, the designer incorporated safeguards against all possible eventualities. The safeguards included not only the usual fuses – much like those used domestically in the home, only larger – but also circuit breakers. These are spring loaded switches which "pop out" under excessive electrical loading, thereby protecting the associated circuit and equipment."

Mr Jones was one of the team flown from Farnborough to Shoreham within an hour of the crash and who over the next few days helped to isolate as much of the electrical material as possible from the wreckage, to send to Farnborough for further analysis. He was then involved in the examination of the material at Farnborough.

"There was an air of supreme urgency as other aeroplanes of the type could have been at risk. Our searching and examinations, along with the work of the electrical design staff at the manufacturer's works, had shortened the list dramatically. It now transpired that if, as we suspected, the circuit breaker had been repeatedly reset, then the consequences must have included the 'blowing' of many fuses, but one in particular – the navigator's station equipment circuit – would really prove the theory. (This was because the electrical supply for the test equipment was taken from the navigator's station circuit).

My priority task became the search for that one fuse to determine if it had 'blown' electrically. The fuse in question was about three quarters of an inch in diameter, and about one and a quarter inches long. It consisted of a heavy ceramic body, with metal end caps, attached by bolts to heavier items known as bus bars. There were many such fuses fitted in banks or rows in the bomber and although originally marked with paint for identification purposes they were broken and now devoid of such identity. They were also mixed with tons of twisted and burnt looms of wire and metal.

My fuse, either intact or in pieces was in the large mound of wreckage now at Farnborough. It was the Whit Monday holiday (May 21st) and I planned an assault on that mound. I had the help of skilled, semi-skilled and unskilled people. The approach was simple. I formed a pyramid of searchers with the unskilled at the mound. They were briefed to sort out all wreckage of a certain character. I made sure they would include more material than I wanted to ensure that the right stuff would come through for searching. Unwanted wreckage was discarded and required material passed back to a second row of helpers who had been briefed in more detail. They in turn passed back this selected material, and so the search continued. Each row of searchers was more qualified to select than the one before, and I was at the apex of the pyramid to make the final decision.

By patience, persistence and careful search and study, we discovered the first of the end caps after only two hours. It was still bolted to a piece of identifiable bus bar, although this itself had been badly damaged. An hour later the other end cap was found. Both caps contained pieces of ceramic body protruding but not mating to make up the body. We found other odd pieces of ceramic and one of these made the link between the end caps: I had my fuse.

I took the end caps to my microscope and there was the evidence that I sought. Traces of fuse wire had been electrically overloaded. The wire ends had formed into globules – a tell-tale sign of a fuse melted by electrical overheating and not by crash fire burning.

We now knew that the electrical supplies in the bomber had been disrupted by the repeated resetting of the circuit breaker – a senseless, illogical action which had led to tragedy and loss of life, including the life of the instigator of the situation. The repeated resetting of the circuit breaker was akin to tackling the symptom and not the cause of the experiment failure.

However, the accident prompted a long hard look at the electrical circuitry of all the large bombers and some shortcomings were brought to light. As I have said on other occasions, regretfully, in aviation someone must suffer, it seems, if aeroplanes are to be made safer."

This conclusion by Mr Jones, that the Ministry of Supply technician Mr Knight was responsible for causing the accident, was reached just 3 days after the conclusion of the Court of Inquiry but was not mentioned at the inquest in Shoreham, held 3 weeks later. Indeed, at the inquest Squadron Leader Finch stated that the primary cause of the crash was electrical failure and that it was in no way connected with the failure of the test equipment. Of course, the Court of Inquiry was not a public inquiry and the documents were marked secret and locked away for over thirty years. They were not released to public viewing until 1988. It would appear that there were no further official reports following the Court of Inquiry, certainly none that I can find on public record. So it seems that the actual cause of the electrical failure may always remain a mystery.

Flight Lieutenant Colin Preece's later account of the crash

John Young, who as an eleven-year-old schoolboy lived in Croft Avenue and heard the explosion, has always remained interested in the crash and many years ago wrote to the co-pilot Colin Preece. He has kindly shared with me the reply he received

"To understand the flying problems experienced in this accident, it is essential to appreciate the difference between flying the Valiant using the power controls, and in the manual reversion mode. Using power the Valiant was a delight to fly, the ailerons and elevators being nicely weighted and balanced, giving a positive response to all inputs. In manual, the exact opposite applied. Both ailerons and elevators were extremely heavy and unresponsive. Manual reversion was, essentially, a get you home feature. The "in service" limitations, I think I'm right in saying, were 190kts IAS, and 20 degrees of bank. These limits were treated with great respect, and flight in manual had to be carefully planned and flown, in the knowledge that each manoeuvre involved considerable effort and time. It was impossible to initiate or terminate any manual change quickly.

Thus, when we were race tracking at around 1500ft and 330kts and heading in an easterly direction, and the controls reverted to manual, the control column was virtually immovable as we were well over 100kts above the limiting speed. The revision occurred without any warning. We had no idea why the power system had failed but knew that it was essential to reduce speed. Ken selected airbrakes "out", but there was no response. Power was then reduced and trim applied to control the nose down pitch. But the variable incidence tailplane was also inoperative. The Valiant continued in this nose down attitude, which could not be controlled despite both pilots having feet up on the instrument panel to gain more purchase on the stick, and crashed in a recreation ground in Southwick. The RAE estimate that I ejected at somewhere between 80 and 120 feet, and I was fortunate to be in a fully automatic seat. At no time did the aircraft climb or drop a wing. Nor was it on fire as one national paper reported. (Almost an inevitable reaction)

As you can appreciate it was essential to know the cause of the accident without delay, and a session in the Valiant simulator confirmed the control problems we had experienced and pointed towards some sort of electrical failure. Subsequent investigations by Vickers indicated that in certain circumstances the four generators would cease to operate, and that, simultaneously, the pilot's four generator warning lights would, due to a design fault, be inoperative.

The likely sequence was seen to be as follows:-the four generators go offline: and at the same time the pilots warning lights are rendered inoperative: the batteries support the electrical loads but are gradually drained: the power controls and other associated systems fail without warning: the aircraft is not controllable in manual at the relatively high speed."

Final Thoughts

When I first read the official crash report the thing that leapt out at me straight away was the poignant radio transmission on the official call log of the flight. Three minutes after take-off from Wisley, Squadron Leader Orman asked "Will you order 3 late lunches". Here were four young men going about their job and expecting to be back in Farnborough for their lunch. Instead three of them returned in coffins to be buried in Ship Lane Cemetery.

The graves of the three crew at Ship Lane Cemetery, Farnborough

Squadron Leader Colin Donald Preece, A.F.C. continued a distinguished career in the Royal Air Force. He had already received the Queen's Commendation for Valuable Service in the Air, in 1955, the year before the Valiant crash. On 1st January 1958, now a Squadron Leader, he was awarded the Air Force Cross. The award is granted for "an act or acts of exemplary gallantry while flying, though not in active operations against the enemy". On 19th December 1961 he again received the Queen's Commendation for Valuable Service in the Air: For outstanding skill and devotion to duty in successfully landing his Valiant aircraft after the elevator controls had jammed. Memories of the Southwick accident must have gone through his mind whilst fighting to land this aircraft. In 1977 he was made an Officer of the Order of the British Empire (OBE) in the New Year Honours.

The answer to what actually caused the crash of Valiant B Mk 1 WP 202 on 11th May 1956 may never be fully known. It seems to me that there are several factors which on their own did not cause the crash, but which may have contributed to it. The pilot decided to fly low to burn up fuel quickly and to stay below the cloud for better visibility. This meant that when the electrics failed, and the controls reverted to manual, the plane became unmanageable. They were flying at over 100kts above the recommended speed for manual flying. The greater air resistance at the lower level and speed meant the ailerons and flaps wouldn't work, even with both pilots putting their feet up on the control panel to pull harder on the controls. Had it been flying much higher there may have been a chance of controlling it. Flying low also meant that the rear crew did not have the time or the height to successfully parachute from the aircraft.

Fred Jones asserts that it was the actions of the civilian flight observer, Mr Knight, constantly resetting the circuit breaker which caused the crash. The constant resetting may have led to a fuse blowing, but it was surely a design failure which allowed one blown fuse to cause the entire electrics of the plane to fail. The Court of Inquiry found that a single fault in any one of several places in the standard Valiant's electrical installation could jeopardise the safety of the aircraft. They also found that there was no proof that the specialist test equipment contributed to the power supply failure and that at the most it may have touched a weak feature in the Valiant's normal electrical system.

From my reading of the investigation reports it appears that the 112V electrical generators failed quite some time before the crash but the reserve 96V battery kicked in, and together with the remaining power in the 28V battery, kept the electrics working. Unfortunately the warning lights, which should have alerted the pilot to the failure of the electrical generators were powered by the generators themselves, rather than the backup battery. So when all four generator circuits failed simultaneously the power warning lights no longer worked, and the crew were unaware that there was a problem until it was too late. The aeroplane controls continued to work normally, meaning the pilots were oblivious to the loss of power, but were draining the batteries. Had the warning lights worked the pilot would no doubt have flown higher and probably out to sea, which would have given them all a chance to escape to safety. As it was, the first the pilot knew of the problem was when the reserve batteries drained and all electrical power was lost. By this time it was too late to do anything as the plane had become unmanageable; a 40-ton lump of metal hurtling at over 350 miles an hour towards Southwick.

Whatever the cause, the sad fact is that the Valiant became uncontrollable and three of the crew tragically lost their lives. The plane could have crashed anywhere as it was completely out of control and heading towards a densely populated area. The miracle was that it crashed on a relatively open space. Despite the fact that it hit a railway line just before a train went along it, causing considerable damage to adjacent houses where wives were preparing lunch, and showering a popular recreation ground and primary school with debris, no one on the ground was killed or even seriously injured.

Glossary

Actuator	An actuator is a component of a machine that is responsible for moving and controlling a mechanism or system, for example by opening a valve.
AIB	Accident Investigation Branch
Ailerons and tail trims	Panels on the wings which allow the pilot to control the movement of the aeroplane.
Bus bar	A metallic strip used to carry large amounts of current
Form 700	A form to record all servicing, modifications, repairs and refuelling carried out on an aircraft.
Forms P1 and P2	The paperwork detailing the alterations for the test
HRC	High Rupturing Capacity
MOS	Ministry of Supply
MOT	Ministry of Transport
MTCA	Ministry of Transport and Civil Aviation
Notice in motion	A motion at Council meetings usually reserved for the election of the chairman and the selection of committees
RAE	Royal Aircraft Establishment
Tufnol	A plastic similar to Bakelite
Very lights	Flare guns
Vickers-Armstrong (Aircraft) Limited	The Valiant manufacturers

Acknowledgements

I am very grateful to all the people who have shared their memories of the event with me.

Alan, Malcolm and Colin Guy, John Young, Mike Peacock, Mike Shoulders, Richard Palmer, and Terry Langrish

Also thank you to the following for their help

David Cross from South East History Boards

Roger Gates

Sue Worrall from Worthing Library

West Sussex Record Office for use of catalogue no. PH 16097

And finally a very special thank you to Barry and Christopher Candy for their patience and help

Sources

"Air Crash" The Clues in the Wreckage by Fred Jones

Aircrew Remembered http://aircrewremembered.com

British Military Aircraft by Chaz Bowyer

Colonel Templer and the birth of aviation at Farnborough, May 2007, Royal Aeronautical Society

Hansard

Local and National Newspapers

London Gazette

South East History Boards

The National Archive

The Southwick Society Archive

UK Military Losses http://www.ukserials.com/losses-1956.htm

V-Bombers by Bob Downey

Whilst many of the photographs reproduced in this book are from the Southwick Society's own collection I would like to thank the following for their kind permission to use their material: Worthing Library, West Sussex Records Office, Neil Aird, and Aircraft Engine Historical Society, Inc., http://www.enginehistory.org. It has not been possible to trace the photographers or original copyright holders of all photographs but their contribution is gratefully acknowledged.

The Southwick (Sussex) Society

The Southwick Society is a local amenity society formed in 1973 to promote interest in Southwick and to work for the enhancement and protection of its environment. As part of its work it has restored the 15th century Manor Cottage in Southwick Street where it has established a local heritage centre. This book is published as part of that project and money raised from its sale will be applied to the work of the Society. Membership is open to anybody interested in Southwick and the Society may be contacted at southwicksociety@gmail.com or at www.southwicksociety.org